FIVE TO FIFTEEN

A Woman, A Prison, A Redemption

By
Denise Sassoon

Five to Fifteen
A Woman, A Prison, A Redemption
Copyright © 2015 Denise Sassoon

Published by
Sasden Press

For publishing and distribution inquires contact:
Sasden Press
For all publishing and PR inquiries contact:
Denise Sassoon at sassoon194@gmail.com

Printed in the United States of America

ISBN-13: 978-0692528587
ISBN-10: 069252858X

Library of Congress Control Number 2014957233

Book design by Drew Bailey

DEDICATION

For my mother, Stephanie, the most tolerant, humble, grateful, and kind-hearted person I've ever known, and for my beloved siblings, Nate, Jonathan, and Jeanette.

And for Joanne, the absolute light and love of my life, who stood by my side for twenty-five years and gave me the rarest treasure—perfect love.

CONTENTS

PART THREE
BIG POND, LITTLE FISH

PART FOUR
BACK TO PRISON

PREFACE

In my life's work, each day has been filled with the inevitable heart-breaks and miracles that go hand-in-hand with trying to demonstrate and instill community among people who rarely, if ever, had it. These are the people most of society does not want to know about or even see, people who have no voice: drug addicts, alcoholics, and ex-convicts. *Five to Fifteen*, which was begun in 1978 with scribbled notes and journals composed inside a dark prison cell, attempts to give them—to give us—a voice.

Advances in communication technology have streamlined transmittal of information, but have depersonalized human-to-human connection. The result has been loss of community and the resurgence of a "me" generation. Our culture's loss of community has had devastating and grave implications for all of us, resulting in alienation, loneliness, and ever-growing pain. It seems that more people than ever are in anguish today—certainly the most I've observed in my lifetime—but have nowhere to go because of rampant social alienation. It is only through community, along with perseverance and development of spiritual strength, that people have hope of balancing excruciating depths of pain with an equal or greater degree of happiness and peace.

I acknowledge here the men and women who have struggled to overcome the agonies of prison time and addiction, and particularly those who have worked selflessly to demonstrate that change is possible. *Five to Fifteen* is a testament to their suffering, courage, and hard-fought battles for better lives.

Over thirty years in the making, *Five to Fifteen* has been edited several times and finally brought into being through the encouragement and specific contributions of several individuals. The first was Kelli Dawn, my dear friend and writer who gave me hope that what I had to say was of value. I am thankful for the editors I hired to assist me with the initial drafts of my manuscript, Connie Whitcraft and Christine Miller. I also thank Jennifer Harris for her generous thought-filled advice, feedback, and contributions to the development of my manuscript. I am thankful to Kathryn Cloward and the Kandon Publishing team for their tireless and generous support, guidance, and wisdom throughout the publishing process. I thank the bounty of friends I have made throughout my life and work, all of whom I respect and admire and to whom I am indebted for their continual love and support. Thank you to my family for giving me permission to share our history, which was not always pleasant, and for standing by me all those years I was unable to stand on my own. Most of all, I thank Joanne—my beloved, departed wife—who gave me everything I could have ever asked for and more.

PART ONE

CONVICT OR INMATE?

CHAPTER 1
Doing Time

1975. September. Sitting inside the caged confines of a government vehicle, I was end-of-week cargo being delivered to the state prison. Outside, through metal webbing, the morning sun was wide awake and splashing its brilliance across the desert scrub. I was inclined simply to stare between my feet and follow the scratched paths embedded into the blue steel floor. The hum of tires holding steady against the asphalt filled any spaces I had left.

I cannot tell you how long it took to get there. The mind seeks sheltering places in moments like these. Time isn't a player, not any longer. And then bump, a slight hitch, and we were through the entry gate of Arizona State Prison for Women.

I was handed over to Sergeant Craig, who greeted me cordially, even warmly. A petite woman with flawless skin, she signed off on the body receipt handed to her by the escorting officer and began to size me up. Her eyes were as cautious as her smile was stiff. Her manner conveyed a practiced if not all-knowing authority to which I would soon become accustomed. This routine, even the warmness, was the finished product of a procedure she had completed too many times for her to regard further.

Sergeant Craig escorted me across the yard, noticeably green and alive with a clipped lawn and smattering of manicured trees—odd, being that a desert had the prison under siege from all sides. Solid block walls and prominent fences topped with triple razor wire threatened back any hope from the sky. A few paces further on, I became aware of the buildings about me that loomed in stark contrast to anything needing to breathe. Bars were on every window and seemingly polished, testimony that nothing rusts in prison but the inmates. Last, I noticed the other prisoners, who stood around in pairs or clusters, wearing uniform jeans and blue shirts that safely spared me any personal details for now. I was not ready to look at them, not with the way they were eying me, assessing my possible utility.

Stopping the brisk tour at a building with a sign that read Dorm 2, Sergeant Craig spoke, but the words didn't register. We entered. I followed her down a corridor with numbered doors on both sides until she stopped in front of one midway—number five—and unlocked it. She tersely stepped aside, gestured in that cordial manner, and ordered, "In."

Once I was inside what appeared to be a holding cell, she held out an institutional rulebook from the Arizona Department of Corrections (*ADOC*). "Read this, do what it says, and we'll get along fine."

As she shut the heavy door behind her, she said she'd be back on Monday to take me to a physical and cavity inspection for contraband, performed by the infirmary nurse.

"The nurse won't be back 'til Monday. You shouldn't have come on a Friday," she remarked, as though I could have made an advance reservation for my arrival.

I knew what they would want to check for in my cavity search. Years before, I had learned about *keestering* drugs. Wildly profitable and fairly simple, keestering was a clever but crude use of one's anal cavity, and for women other cavities, to smuggle drugs and paraphernalia. I knew of instances where people even keestered syringes. Left alone in the cell, I considered the stupidity of the prison staff. As if anything in my cavities would still be there by Monday if I'd been fortunate enough to have drugs!

Later, I began reading the rulebook, called *ADOC Title 15*. It was structured like a law book with statutes and number–letter codes. The rules ranged from no horseplay or physical contact to no assault or murder. The penalties for violating codes included verbal warnings, new charges, and indeterminate administrative segregation, or "hole time," about which I would soon become intimately knowledgeable.

A tiny window high on the cell door allowed me to peer out to the long, narrow hallway lined with eight cells on either side. I spent most of the weekend listening to muffled female voices that seeped in through the cracks of the cell door. There were about ten women with odd names I had never heard: Dusty, Maggot, Bon, Shorty, Dink, and Red. One was named Julie, but they called her Say Snitch. When I could make out what they were saying, the gist of the conversations was mainly about who was doing what to whom and what their plans were for the weekend. When I heard them talking about me, the new girl in number five who had gotten five years, my ears perked up. How did they know anything about my sentence? Feeling so alone, I really wanted to join in the conversations, but fear held me back. My mind kept returning to that sentencing day in the courtroom and my shock when the judge proclaimed "no less than five, no more than fifteen years." Later, I learned that the law I had been sentenced under was only months old, a mandatory drug law enacted during a critical election year. To seal my fate, the judge who had been assigned my case, Alice Truman, happened to be what many referred to as a "hanging judge." Not only that, I discovered I had been tricked by my own public defender to plead guilty.

In the predictable paradox of drug use, I desperately wished for a fix of something, anything, even though the habit had led to my undoing in the first place, landing me here in this miserable place. I gazed out another small window in my cell trying to remember the world outside. It revealed the yard and a building that housed inmates whose faces I could see peering out their windows. From what I could see, unlike the dorm I was in with individual cells, it had small cubicles divided by short, ceramic-looking walls. Each cubicle had a dresser and tiny, metal twin bed. Even though this arrangement seemed more open, the lives of the women held there were shut inside, as mine now was at just 21 years old.

By Monday morning, slowing building panic had begun to settle in my chest, and I felt like I couldn't breathe. Trying to regain some composure, I focused on the view out the window. Today I would have to face these people. The key sounding in the door interrupted the racing mania of my thoughts, and in strode Sergeant Craig to accompany me to the infirmary.

She was seamlessly pleasant, even on a Monday morning.

"C'mon girl, get yourself dressed and we can get you off lock-down today," she said perkily as she exited and stood outside to wait for me.

"I'll be ready in five minutes," I answered, trying to cover the shakiness in my voice. While I dressed, fear slithered down to the pit of my stomach. It might just as well have been a violent desert monsoon storm on the other side of that cell door.

When Sergeant Craig unlocked the door a second time, the words of a girl I had met in the county jail during the week I spent there just before "pulling chain" suddenly came to me. "Don't take nuthin' from nobody and min' yo' own business," she had advised. How ironic that the term used for gang rape, pulling chain, was the same term used for transporting a prisoner from county jail to state or federal prison.

As I pondered those words, I remembered that on my first night here, a girl named Josie, whom I had known years earlier in juvenile hall, came by my cell to ask if I needed anything. Without hesitation, I had told her I needed cigarettes, and in minutes, she slid five of them under my cell door. Remembering those cigarettes, I realized I had already violated that earlier advice. I was probably screwed.

I tried to say good morning to Sergeant Craig, but by this time couldn't speak at all. I was sweating and my legs were shaking. There was an unfamiliar sensation shooting through them, as though they were no longer attached to me.

I followed her down the hall toward the door that led out to the yard. Nearby, a woman in prison clothes was mopping the floor.

"Bon, this is Denise, a new inmate," Sergeant Craig announced, her voice echoing through the dorm. "She'll be moving into cell number five today."

"Uh, hi," I said uneasily.

"How ya doin'," she mumbled, without as much as a glance at Sergeant Craig or me. I felt immediately intimidated by Bon. She was a tall, thin woman with dirty-blond, shoulder-length hair, and a freckled fair face and looked to be in her late 20s. Her demeanor sent the clear message, "Don't fuck with me."

The metal door slammed behind Sergeant Craig and me as we walked outside, after which the Arizona sun resumed its blindingly bright reflection on the steel.

As Sergeant Craig escorted me through the yard, I noticed cottonwood trees growing on an emerald lawn, a baseball diamond, a track, and a ramada with eight stone picnic tables under it. Strange how closely it resembled a park.

"Nice yard," I said meagerly, attempting to break the thick air made even heavier with silence.

"It is, isn't it? You might feel different by next week though," she replied dryly, all-business now. "The yard is every new inmate's first job assignment. You'll start working as soon as you leave the infirmary."

As we continued along, I noticed many pairs of eyes glaring at me: cold, sad, vicious, and curious. Mine were lowered, afraid to meet any of them. Sergeant Craig was going on about some ten-cents-an-hour wage I would earn working in the yard. I only half-heard her. My attention had been captured by a stout Indian woman with a Marine-style crew cut, wearing men's trousers and a flawlessly ironed and creased men's shirt, with black, wing-tipped shoes. Her size, hair, dress, and mannerisms nearly erased her identity as a woman, but large, drooping breasts were startling evidence that she was.

"Say, Dusty, ya' gonna be around the laundry later?" yelled someone from across the yard. The Indian woman, apparently Dusty, answered. Her voice and name matched one of those I had heard from inside my holding cell. Again I felt a sudden rush of panic, like a siren going off in my head.

We made it to the infirmary, where two other women in a small reception room occupied the only chairs, metal-constructed and bolted to the floor. To my relief, Sergeant Craig skipped the introductions this time. Already the faces, names, and voices buzzing in my head and blurring my vision.

The nurse looked well past sixty years old. Like someone caught in a time warp, she had tired-looking, wiry, white hair and horn-rimmed glasses she might have purchased in the 1950s. She scurried about busily and with an air of authority, in and out of tiny examining rooms.

Sergeant Craig stopped her. "This is a new inmate. Can you see her now?"

"Yes, yes, she'll just need to wait a few minutes," the nurse replied abruptly, turning away impatiently.

So wait I did, but without a place to sit, I felt like an exhibit in a display case. I was thankful, however, that I was soon ordered to an examining room. Cringing at the idea of the nurse's old, bony fingers probing my cavities, I sat down reluctantly on the examining table.

She told me to undress, saying she'd return shortly. I did as I was told, undressing and putting on the thin gown she'd handed given me. Sweat soaked through the material as I waited, keeping my eyes averted from the cold stirrups at the end of the table.

The nurse reappeared and demanded my name. Clearly, there would be no small talk to put me at ease.

"Denise."

"Lie down," she ordered, looking hurried and slightly agitated. "I will be doing a cavity check, a pap smear, and a physical."

I leaned back and began to consider that five years of pap smears, which I had always hated, might be easier than facing the inmates once I left the infirmary. But pap smears don't last five years, and people don't usually get five years on their first conviction. Or was it fifteen? "No less than five, no more than fifteen." I could still see the judge's stone-cold eyes as she banged her gavel.

I tried to translate these numbers into actual years that I would have to stay in this place. I couldn't. I had heard in the jail about good time, flat time, and two for one time, but initially had no idea how these might apply to my sentence. Neither the attorney nor the judge had explained the terms to me. Most of what I needed to know came later, from the convicts. They taught me that "good time" meant the same thing as "two for one time." For every day in prison, one day of credit is given if one behaves, reducing most sentences by half. Of course, this didn't apply if one got "flat time," like my sentence. In this case, five years meant five years.

"If you would just relax, the examination would get done a lot sooner," the nurse snapped. Yeah, I thought, when was the last time you had bony fingers up your ass or a speculum up your vagina?

"I'm sorry. I've always hated pap smears," I said.

"I was almost finished anyway," she shot back. "You can dress now and wait in the lobby for the sergeant."

Sergeant Craig came promptly and led me outside to the prison yard world of grass, sand, blazing sun, and barbed wire. It was 100 degrees outside, not unusual for Arizona in September. She told me I was now officially on the yard crew and left me in what was called the sand trap, a six-foot-wide strip of sand in between a block wall and a chain-link fence topped with razor wire.

Seven or eight women, all giving me sizing-up glances, were pulling weeds. I joined them. The weeds were as tall as my waist. Ms. Hatton, an old, fat, hick-sounding woman with short, white, curly hair, supervised us. Her tired manner and gait drew a raw portrait of age, neglect, and indifference.

"Hey, Cuca, d'ya hear 'bout Sonya gettin' busted for sugar? They thought it was crystal meth, said the lab report even confirmed it," a black woman remarked. "Are you ready for that shit?"

"I can believe it. I sho' can," said another woman.

"Time for count, ladies," Ms. Hatton broke in. I didn't know what "count" meant and was afraid to ask. I decided to follow the others. I helped pick up rakes and hoes, and we walked toward a dilapidated tool shed with spider webs covering the door. The rest of the crew threw their tools to the ground outside the shed door and walked off as two of the convicts abruptly ordered me to put them away. I did.

In that instant, I was suddenly overwhelmed with a sense of the disconnection between me and the harsh reality of what I'd be facing for the next five years. This was just one of many startling, somewhat surreal moments I would experience over this time.

"I said, it's count time, lady." Ms. Hatton glared at me with aggravation.

"Count?" I asked, nearly jumping through the roof of the shed and dropping the tools.

"Yes, count," she said. "It's time to go to your dorm and line up in front of your house for count. Then you'll get lunch and come back to work. And you can't talk during count. Get a move on, now."

I was thinking, walking, and trying to get a grip on reality. I felt like Sally Field in the movie *Sybil*, in which she played a young schizophrenic girl. In one scene, she walks, talks, and walks some more, then screams, grunts, and finally runs frantically and aimlessly down the street.

Somehow I made it to the dorm, and a wholesome-looking young woman in a blue-and-white uniform opened the door and let me in. Pinned proudly onto her breast was a badge that read CORRECTIONAL OFFICER WOODARD. Her beauty—she had shining, brown hair, a firm figure, and a face and complexion I can only describe as radiant—coupled with the refreshing, energetic way about her brightened my bleak thoughts for a moment.

I faced inmates who lined the halls on both sides in front of each cell, or house, as I had heard them call it. I thought it was pretty strange to refer to cells as houses. I kept my head lowered and stared at the floor. It was as though the tiles were a force-field drawing my eyes downward.

At number five stood a young girl with long, blond hair and an inno-cent-looking face. She had an anxious way about her, a deer-caught-in-the-headlights look in her eyes.

"Hi," she nearly whispered, "I'm Julie. I guess you are moving into my house."

"Yeah, they said number five," I replied.

Julie, I thought to myself, was the one called Say Snitch. I wasn't sure, but I didn't think it was the best thing to be her roommate, or cellie (another new word in prison vocabulary I would soon learn). Her hands fidgeted nervously and her voice quivered.

"I think something is coming down in the dorm today," she said.

"Like what?" I asked.

"I don't know. I just have a bad feeling," she replied. "You wouldn't believe how scary it is in here. I'm so glad I get out in four months. What about you? How much time did you get?"

"Five years, I guess, but I'm not sure 'cause the judge said five to fifteen," I told her.

"Oh, my God," she exclaimed. "You poor thing. Uh, oh, c'mon, it's time to line up to go to chow."

In the chow hall, I was the last in a line of over a hundred women. Julie asked me to sit with her and I declined, recalling her Say Snitch inmate status. My eyes dared not meet anyone's gaze, and I sat very still, but underneath the table the whole lower half of my body was shaking. I tried to be invisible. No one talked to me, but I could feel hundreds of eyes watching every move I made. The stench of sweaty convicts' bodies and greasy food odors hung in the air. It nauseated me to even look at my plate.

After count and lunch, I pulled weeds again, wondering about my dorm mates. I thought of the tension that Julie mentioned. Perhaps she was right. Something was coming down. Shit! Maybe they're after me. My mind rioted. I pulled weeds faster.

"Say, is yo' ancestors black or sumpthin'? Boogie, d'ya see dis white girl's nappy hair?" said a huge, black woman. I had tried everything that existed to straighten my hair, especially throughout the 1960s when long straight hair was the norm, but it remained stubbornly nappy most of my life. When I let it grow out, it had a mind of its own and formed an Angela Davis–like Afro. I said nothing. The black woman strutted across the yard, shaking her head.

At quitting time, I walked toward my dorm and hoped for sanctuary in my house. A different corrections officer opened the door from the outside, but this time after she let me in, she left the dorm and all the house doors unlocked. Then she walked off, headed toward the chow hall.

A woman with bright-red hair, blue eyes, and a face full of freckles stood by the dayroom window that faced the yard and kitchen. She was one of my dorm mates. Hardly looking at me, she directed, "Get to your house, close your door, and stay there 'til we tell ya to come out." I couldn't walk fast enough.

My house offered no sanctuary. It felt like the walls were closing in, and the very air forbade me to move. I was trapped and knew they would get me soon. For an hour, my thoughts were stuck on death or worse. I heard them scuttling back and forth in the hall. If they were going to beat up on me, why didn't they just do it and get it over with?

Two hours later, another corrections officer came in to announce count. I was safe for a few moments. After count was clear, it was dinnertime. Unlike lunch and breakfast, however, this meal was not mandatory to attend. I blindly chose to remain inside, preferring to get it over with, whatever "it" was.

The corrections officer left and most of the inmates stayed. I was alone with them, my ill fate looming. But no one paid any attention to me. I began to consider the remote possibility that something was going on, but that it was not about me. Maybe they were shooting dope or smoking pot or beating someone up and just didn't want me to know. I crouched in my cell and prayed to the god I had denounced so many years before, after one of my stepfathers had raped me and my mother had retreated into silent denial. Prayer was foreign to me, but on this day, in this moment, I prayed hard.

I looked up to my small window, which at the moment was framing the redhead's pretty face. She told me to go to the front day room window to pin for the cops. Phew, I sighed to myself with unimaginable relief, they aren't after me. Though I didn't know what "pin" meant, I surmised it had to do with being a lookout. Turned out I was right.

I stood by the window for two hours, along with other lookouts stationed by the windows of the dorms across the way. We were like a silent army. Fifty or more windows, all with faces peering out: intense, patient, watchful, and united. Some convicts were playing softball in the distance. I couldn't help noticing the oppressive, yet beautiful monsoon clouds hanging above them. Looking at the clouds, I felt relief and sadness wash over me at the same time. I still didn't know what was going on and didn't really care. I was safe for the time being.

Dusty unlocked a door at the back end of the hallway with a key she pulled from her pocket.

"Jesus Christ!" I whispered to myself. "It's an escape!"

The back door was three or four feet from the chain-link fence and sand trap we had been in earlier. Beyond that was freedom. The redhead was on her hands and knees in the sand trap. An old, unkempt, hunched-over, sort of pathetic-looking woman with gray-black, greasy hair climbed up onto her back, while two other women hoisted her over the wall. Once over the razor wire—two women had thrown gray, state-issue blankets high enough to cover a section of the wire—the escapee faded away out of sight into the barren desert.

The redhead crawled back through the hole they had cut in the fence and covered the foot and handprints left in the sand. She came back into the dorm, and Dusty relocked and closed the door triumphantly. They shared a smile and motioned to the crowd of faces in the windows that all was clear.

At 8:00 we stood by our houses, snickering and giggling like first graders at a slumber party, as we watched the police go mad because they couldn't clear count. A clear count meant we were all still in prison and accounted for. They finally realized there had been an escape and that Betty Smithey was missing. We had to stand in front of our houses for three hours, but it didn't matter because we were giddy, united, and full of ourselves for the brilliant escape we had just helped pull off.

The redhead approached me later and said, "Hey, thanks for your help and for keepin' your mouth shut. My name is Judi."

"No problem," I replied. "I'm Denise."

"Wasn't that a bitchin' escape? I'm so glad we got Betty out. She's doing natural life, ya know. She's already done fourteen years."

"Oh yeah, what's she in for?" I asked.

"Murder. She strangled a fifteen-month-old baby back in '63. She was twenty years old, babysitting," Judi answered.

Oddly, even though baby-killers tend to do very hard time in prison, Betty didn't. During her trial, her lawyer argued that she was mentally ill and that she had suffered a turbulent childhood. Her father had died when she was four years old, and the state declared her poverty-stricken mother was incapable of caring for her seven daughters. All the children had become wards of the state and were separated, most of them never seeing each other again. At eight years old, Betty had begun the journey that so many displaced children travel, through the foster care system. The victim of abuse over several years by various foster parents, she suffered psychological trauma and ill health. At the prison, it was obvious to everyone that Betty just wasn't "all there."

"Fourteen years is just too much time for anybody to do. She has natural life. What's she got to lose, right?" I asked what she meant by natural life. She explained that it meant life without the possibility of parole.

"Yeah, I suppose you're right," I said. "Hey, how'd you guys cut the hole in the fence?"

"It wasn't easy," boasted Judi. "We've been cutting for weeks. My ole' man smuggled the wire cutters in through the mailroom in the back of my TV. The police will never figure this one out. The hardest thing about getting away with anything is tryin' to keep the inmates from running their mouths. Most of 'em are worse than the police."

"I'll remember that," I said.

"Hey, gotta go," she told me. "Thanks again, see ya 'round."

"Sure thing," I said.

Three days passed. I was calmer. I walked the yard feeling sad for Betty. She turned herself back in the morning after the escape because she got cold and hungry in the desert. Someone told me she dragged her head across her isolation cell until it bled. What an irony to call her term natural life. To me, there was absolutely nothing natural about the life here.

***

The months went by, and I adjusted. Living in prison got easier, but still felt surreal. I quickly learned that the difference between a convict and an inmate was immensely important. And that the bottom line—whether you did easy or hard time in prison—was decided by whether you passed or failed a series of tests. Like every other fish, or new person, I had to pass the tests: tests of whether I would stand up for myself, tests of my will to survive, tests of whether I would snitch, and most importantly, the ultimate test of whether I was a convict or an inmate.

Convicts had anything they wanted or needed by taking everything the inmates had through use of force, brutality, extortion, and/or intimidation. The convicts owned the inmates. Inmates could be bought, sold, or traded for a pack of cigarettes. Once deemed weak by the convicts, an inmate's fate was uncertain. That lesser status sometimes forced them to pay a chilling price.

The tests were unwritten, but definitely understood by everyone except the person faced with taking them. One just had to figure it out. I passed the first test when I helped with Betty's escape. More tests would come, I was certain.

As it turned out, the dorm I resided in was a max, or maximum-security dorm. The women who lived there had staged a riot the summer before and the National Guard had been called in to regain control of them, bashing their heads in with billy clubs. Those women were convicts! The coincidence of my arriving late on a Friday after the nurse had left, and thus being placed in the max dorm, is probably what saved me from being thought of as an inmate. This dorm housed women who wouldn't allow themselves to be associated with anyone who wasn't a convict, and if this meant they had to take me under their collective wing and teach me the prison codes, they would do so. Over the next few months, I was a willing student who learned quickly.

After a few months working in the yard, I got a better paying job in the kitchen. I had to get up at 3:30 a.m., but I liked it. Before daybreak it was quiet, no prison sounds. Working in the kitchen was considered a good pay number—better wages for the work—and had its perks.

We were innovative. Between the commissary and stolen kitchen food, we produced three- and four-course dinners using popcorn poppers and irons. And we almost always had a ready supply of hooch (homemade liquor), which took six to eight weeks to ferment. We hid it in the attic of the dorms or inside closets in the chapel. It was made using rice, potatoes, fruit, and sugar and was strained using thin socks or nylons. The smell and taste of it were overpowering and disgusting, but hard as it was to drink, it was 80-proof alcohol and did the trick.

CHAPTER 2
Coming Out

Another test in prison concerns homosexuality. Homosexuality runs rampant in prison, and every woman sent there has a decision to make: whether she will engage or not. Intimacy with the same sex is deeply embedded in prison culture.

"I bet two cartons of cigarettes you'll be out in six months," a woman named Carol said to me pointedly. I'd made her acquaintance within my first few months in prison. She'd done so much speed that her face twitched on its own.

"No way, not for me," I responded emphatically. I expounded to anyone who would listen that I never had and never would sleep with a woman. In my mind, the women around me who were engaging in homosexuality were sick and disgusting, and even though it appeared that they were willing participants, I was sure they had been forced or beaten into submission behind closed doors. I had also convinced myself that those uneasy feelings I once had had for a girl named Leslie—my best friend in the fourth grade—were unnatural, knowing at the time that if I allowed myself to think otherwise, I was bound for hell.

I was to prove myself wrong, however, and Carol right. My outspoken, adamant defense of my heterosexuality was a symptom of my inner resistance to an idea highly forbidden and terrifying, and yet somehow enticing. It seems that in this area, being forced to be around no one but other women daily and constantly was something of a blessing in the end. In the extreme and unnatural environment of prison, I was forced to come to terms with my true sexuality. Had I been "outside," who knows how many men I would have slept with to shore up my denial of preferring intimacy with women. This denial could only serve to deprive me of true sexual and emotional satisfaction anyway.

So along came Judi, with her fiery red hair, azure eyes, and beautiful figure, one of the first to initiate me into prison culture by enlisting my help with Betty's escape. She lived in the cell directly across the hall from mine, and because this dorm had cells instead of cubicles, having sex was very easy. It seemed as though the whole dorm was doing it, with the women taking turns watching for other couples. Prison love was strictly against regulations and therefore secretive by necessity. Administration-wise, getting caught holding hands warranted five days in the hole, or isolation cell. For sex it was thirty days.

Each cell had a bunk bed and held two women. One early morning, Judi was lying in her bed and invited me in for coffee. She lay their smiling, patting the empty side of the bed and gesturing for me to lie down with her. That first kiss was like nothing I had ever felt: soft, easy, luscious, and right. She asked her cellmate to leave the cell and keep watch for us. We then made love, as blissful, sweet, and exciting as it had been with my first man, or rather boy. Sex with men was great, but this was something so astounding, wondrous, perfect, and different that I could never be as I had before. We were both young, only twenty-one, but my feelings for this woman, magical and dangerous, displaced my subconscious awareness of the bleak and dreary years that lay ahead. The irony of starting a five-year prison term and falling more in love than I could have imagined taught me the great breadth and depth of human emotions. It was a crash course in intimacy. How bittersweet that women could experience love of such intensity in this place where so much hate existed: hate for each other, themselves, the system.

I later realized that these relationships were distorted, in part, because they happened during institutionalization, hardly a natural or normal setting.

Sleeping with a woman did not feel foreign or wrong to me. It fit. Judi was one of my first two loves, who both linger sweetly in my heart and always will. My first love was Steve, a hippie-type cowboy I'd known in the 1960s, my high school sweetheart. Judi was the second, but my first time with a woman. I was her first as well. I'll always be grateful for these precious, early relationships, despite how they wound up.

***

Judi and her husband, Mark, had been convicted of armed robbery of a drugstore. The drugstore owner had unexpectedly kept a gun on hand and Mark, in a panic, pushed him through a plate glass window. The man had become paralyzed. Their case made *Parade* magazine.

Mark was a four-time loser, meaning he had been to prison four times, and as often the case, his old lady took the rap. He waited until she was found guilty at trial, pled to a lesser charge, and got five years. She appeared before Judge Sandra Day O'Conner, who was then a presiding Superior Court criminal judge in Phoenix. Judi's sentence was three life terms.

What made my relationship with Judi even more risky and thrilling was that Mark was housed in the Men's Division, which was separated from the Women's Division by a one-lane country road. The Men's Division often sent convict crews to do all those "manly" tasks that women were presumed to be incapable of, such as plumbing, carpentry, and electrical work. In contrast, women were offered educational programs involving culinary and secretarial skills, courses to complete a General Education Degree, and some junior college classes taught by professors who came in from a nearby community college.

Mark was an electrician and often came to the Women's Division with the crews. His reputation preceded him: a real "bad ass." Every one of the 160 women in our compound knew it would be disastrous for Judi if he ever found out she was with a woman. A conspiracy and vow of silence among all the convicts kept him from ever finding out.

Judi and I became an established couple, and from her I learned to do time. She taught me all the ins and outs: how to make love, fool the guards, and brew hooch and where to get enough drugs to stay high (thanks to the stashes inside tennis balls thrown over the wall from the Men's Division nearly every day).

The fact that Judi was serving three life sentences afforded her the same clout that most lifers enjoyed. By virtue of their sentences, respect was a "given" for most lifers, their sentences perhaps humbling for the rest of us? We would one day walk out! From the perspective of the other prisoners and my own, it was beneficial to know a lifer. Judi's request of me to help watch during Betty's escape began my rite of passage from inmate to convict status. Had I chosen not to participate, I would have been relegated to the bottom position in the brutal pecking order of prison society.

Before prison and the chance circumstance of being regarded as a convict, I had mostly been a victim of sorts, or at least, lacking in confidence. Honestly, I don't know which did more damage to my soul, being victim or victimizer. But in prison there was little in between the two. You were one or the other. I got schooled quickly, and almost too easily became a victimizer.

My transformation to convict again surfaced in a situation involving an inmate named Josie. There were one or two major dope connections "on the yard," meaning anywhere in the prison, not necessarily in the outside yard. Judi, Josie, a few select others, and I always knew when there was dope, which was most typically on visiting days (aside from the drugs that came to us from the Men's Division). Visitors of the inmates were allowed two kisses, one at the beginning of the visit and one at the end. Drugs were passed during these important preplanned kisses.

During one such weekend, Josie made the mistake of letting either too many or the wrong people know who was holding the bag, and her punishment came swiftly and severely. My role was to help pin while two other women tied Josie using her own long, thick hair, so black it almost looked blue, to the hot water faucet of a deep laundry sink outside dorm one. They turned the hot water on and left it running. I stood with the others, silent and unmoved, while the hot water scorched Josie's face and neck, resulting in second-degree burns. Her hair had to be cut off to free her from the faucet.

This event and many other violent and abhorrent ones took me far away from myself, and my heart eventually felt as though it had turned to stone. At this point, I began to record my life on paper. I don't think the reality of my five-year term hit me until about two years into it, but certainly, those tests that secured my convict status made it real. The tests would continue, I knew, but I was growing confident that I could pass them. And the fact that Judi's sentence meant she wouldn't be leaving prison except in a coffin helped. I had a release date and a partner.

Doing time was sometimes glorious, other times horrific, but always intense. Being in love, getting high, listening to music, and making friends were the glorious parts. The violence I witnessed daily defined the horrific and intense aspects. Strangely, though, it was also like coming home, in the best sense of the word. My childhood had been chaotic, violent, oppressive, and confusing, so as I adjusted to this bizarre place, it began to fit. I had been in juvenile prison for a year at age seventeen and on the streets doing drugs for nearly ten years by then. My history had made prison the next logical step, given my lifestyle. I was primed for it. Years later, when I tried to describe prison to others, I recounted only the most entertaining vignettes and glamorized my time there. The harrowing details surfaced much later, as I had buried them deep in some remote corner of my mind and body, next to all the demons of my childhood.

***

On my twenty-second birthday, I was out in the yard with a few home girls. Fleetwood Mac's "Rumors" was blaring on a boom box. Stevie Nicks was our hero and made us all feel like "Gold Dust Women." Even the Black and Hispanic girls liked her.

The yard was huge. Inmates and convicts sat in racially segregated groups on the same state-issued gray blankets that had helped Betty get over the razor wire without too many cuts. Each group played its own ethnic music, and the loudest and best stereo prevailed. Usually one of our stereos, my home girls' or mine, was right up there with the best of them.

I took my place on the blanket with Judi and Dink, a good friend of ours. Dink says to me, "Close your eyes and open your mouth." When I did, she put a tab of orange sunshine acid under my tongue. Not only that, a fresh batch of hooch had been brewed in my honor.

It was a grand day. My home girls had made presents for my house— hand-crocheted blankets and beautifully hand-embroidered pillow cases— and gave me eight-track cassette tapes ordered from catalogs. It was one of very few times in my life I felt loved, wanted, respected, and part of something, even though I wasn't yet sure of what. This group of fellow prisoners was the first semblance of what I thought family should be.

In this harsh, violent, bigoted place, there was an indescribable bond among the women. In a way, being in prison is like going to war, albeit on a smaller scale. You have to stand together, fight for your life, and try to come out intact. Some didn't. One such incident involved a marked snitch who cut her own tongue out. She had learned that someone had been ordered to do it, and so decided to do it herself rather than have it done to her. Others hanged themselves. Some had objects forced inside them by angry mobs of young, jaded women. Others took sleeping pills and tranquilizers to numb themselves and sleep their time away. Some became insane years before anyone knew about mental illness. Some got to do plenty of drugs, almost every day, especially pot. Others didn't. Some were taken behind buildings every day and beaten. Others gave the beatings. All, without question, were victims of some kind of war and were forever changed.

Most of the violence in prison had to do with race, drugs, money, and relationships. Domestic violence ran rampant there before the term even came into use. It didn't take long to learn that most of the women were in relationships and participated in this uncanny, yet familiar dynamic that was like a bastardized version of the 1950s nuclear family.

Most couples consisted of a very feminine woman and a very masculine one. Along with this, however, were extended families including aunts, uncles, children, grandmothers, and grandfathers. The rules and roles were clear. Butch women had affairs and beat their women, which were expected of them, even applauded. Her women were expected to iron, cook, pander to, and obey her. The more women a butch had, the more desirable she was. Butch women actually referred to their hard or soft dicks late at night in the dark for all to hear. Such language was probably not the impetus for good dreams, but rather was for the nightmares of countless young and terrified women.

The classic butch women saw themselves as, and were regarded as, "real" men with male names, clothes, tempers, and fists. Of those in relationships (at least eighty percent), most weren't lesbians and would resume their heterosexual lives when they paroled.

Judi and I, as much as possible, didn't agree or buy into the prison version of homosexuality. In fact, this sick structure was precisely why I wasn't with men. I wanted no part of living or being cast into a life defined for me by religion, society, family, anyone! Before then, I had been very conflicted about my sexuality, always fantasizing that I would someday be with a woman and at the same time disgusted and frightened by my own thoughts. I wanted simply to be with someone who would allow me emotional and intellectual equality. It was hard to find men who knew how to let women be who they wanted to be. I had tried, unsuccessfully.

Sex was secondary to me, even though I loved it with men and women. I much preferred to talk, to explore my lovers' minds and souls.

CHAPTER 3
The Hole

Before I hooked up with Judi, I met a girl named Pat from dorm three. She seemed nice enough, even loaning me her radio. Soon after this, fellow convicts noticed that we were friendly. "What the fuck are you doing, hanging with her?" my dorm mates asked. "She's a snitch."

Reportedly, Pat had turned state's evidence against her co-defendant. He was across the street at the Men's Division, serving eighty years. By then I knew to listen to my dorm mates, who were wise in the ways of doing time. In a show of boldness, I even took their advice a step further and decided to keep her radio. I would show her!

This would be my second lesson about lifers and natural life. Most snitches have someone protecting them, and often, it is a lifer. Pat, of course, was no exception. Her protector was Frankie, a huge, hardened lifer who had done twenty-three years inside. Shit.

"You'd best give her radio back," Frankie ordered me. I told her no, but then didn't know what to do after Frankie threatened me. I asked Dink, who had become one of my mentors.

Dink told me, "Baby, you can't give the radio back, and if Frankie comes for you, no matter what you gotta fight. Doesn't matter even whether you win or lose. You gotta fight, earn your stripes."

I knew then that my fate was sealed. There was no way I could beat Frankie in a fight. I was a hippie, for Christ's sake—a child, product, and victim of that 1960s peace, love, and freedom era before the violence arose. Besides that, I was only 5'2" and 110 pounds. Frankie was three times my size and certainly no one to mess with.

I never knew why she didn't come after me, but she didn't. So again by sheer luck, I passed another test. And I had a radio.

One day after work, walking back to my dorm, I passed by two black women walking toward me in the opposite direction. After they passed, one of them—Sondra—turned around and yelled, "Bitch, if you ever step on my foot again, I'll kill you."

I hadn't stepped on her foot and I retorted, "Bitch, I didn't step on your foot," and kept walking. Another of the new lessons I was being schooled in. You don't let anyone disrespect you. If they come at you wrong, well, you come back wrong too.

The next day, she and her home girls approached me in the back of the kitchen. Sondra started calling me names, her big lips moving fast. She was so enraged that she spit at me as she yelled, all the while pointing her finger at me. I could take just about anything, but when someone pointed a finger at me, it unnerved me. It was one of my pet peeves. I had a tray full of bowls of canned pears for the lunch line and, without hesitation or thought of the consequences, heaved it at her.

The kitchen officer didn't see me throw the pears, but heard the clamor and came over. Standing between both of us, she barked, "Break it up NOW and get back to work or you are both going to the warden's office."

I finished working lunch, left the kitchen, and headed toward the yard. Sondra and her home girls met me again, but this time mine were there too. She started screaming obscenities at me, and in the heat of the moment, I called her a "nigger," a word I'd picked up from the ignorant vocabulary of one of my stepfathers. I thought I had long since forgotten it, and I knew better than to repeat the bigotry rampant in my childhood home. Nevertheless, the word slipped out like a reflex.

Because Sondra had called me a "white honky peckerwood," I felt justified in reciprocating with similar hateful verbiage, obligated almost. But with this, another code of prison interaction had been violated. Soon we were screaming in each other's faces and surrounded by a crowd. The yard officers heard the ruckus and came running. They broke us up and escorted us to the warden's office.

The associate warden told us, "Knock off the bullshit right now and apologize to each other," then added that if any more trouble arose from the altercation, we were both going to the hole. The administrators got nervous with racial tension. Sondra and I apologized to each other and promised there would be no more problems on the yard.

I thought it was over, but no such luck. Every time a black girl crossed my path for the next few days, I received a threat. One of those came from a woman named Gracie, who looked me in the eye and said, "Bitch, if it was me, I would have cut your throat. I might anyway." She was serious, and I found out she was the leader of a plot to terrorize me for calling Sondra a "nigger" on the yard.

Every Friday, a truck from the main kitchen in the Men's Division came with a big block of ice and left it on the kitchen loading dock. We were allowed to check out a hammer and ice pick from the kitchen officer and chop ice to take back to our houses for the Styrofoam ice chests filled with soda that we purchased from the commissary. On a Friday around that time, I was washing dishes in a remote corner in the back of the kitchen. Suddenly, I caught Gracie's reflection in the chrome of the sink as she briskly stalked toward me with an ice pick in her hand! I knew it was over. She approached me, stopped, and glared at me for a moment, her look penetrating me. I didn't move. I didn't speak. I'm not sure I even breathed. Just waited. Nothing to do but wait in paralyzed fear. The fact that it was Friday and Gracie was getting ice, escaped me completely. She blasted me with a stare of pure hatred, as if to say, "I'll get you later," and then turned around and left.

The next day after I got off work, I was sleeping in my house. Officer Woodard awoke me to give me a pass to get a package I had waiting in the mailroom. After retrieving the package and heading back toward my dorm, Sondra was waiting for me. As I got closer, she reached out, grabbed my hair, pulled me to the ground, and started punching me in the face. I flailed my arms around, trying to block the blows and free my hair from her grip. It was all I could do to protect myself, much less hit her back. I don't remember much after that as I blacked out, but my home girls told me later that I got the best of her.

The yard officers came, broke us up, and took us both to the hole. We each got thirty days. When there was a fight, no matter who the aggressor was, both people got locked down.

But in another of life's ironies, during those thirty days in the hole together, it was Sondra who taught me how to do "hole time." From her I learned how to make lines, an ingenious method of braiding threads from our sheets and clothes into string that could be slid under the crack at the bottom of the cell door, across the floor, and into a neigh-boring cell. Using the lines, we could play cards while locked in our respective cells. Sondra also showed me what exercises to do while in isolation. She taught me how to get kites (notes and letters from other women on the yard), various necessities, tobacco, pot, and books, in and out. In the end, Sondra and I had bonded.

In the hole, I also met Big Lou, who had been there for eight months. No one was sure what she had done to warrant this lengthy sentence to the hole. The jail officials sometimes used the hole, in addition to psychotropic drugs, to control those who would otherwise be disruptive or violent. They had Big Lou on Thorazine, which she got several times a day.

I would be in and out of the hole over the coming months, so I was witness to Big Lou's moving away from herself and reality. In the mid-dle of the night, she was in her cell with people only she could see. One was her long-lost father, with whom she had screaming fights. Her cries would awaken me from my sleep. Listening to Big Lou's descent into madness, echoing out of her isolation cell window to the dark, empty yard outside, is a memory that has never left me.

***

The hole is a perfect place for deep, gripping conversation. Sondra hadn't been down—in prison, that is—very long either. We talked at great length about how we had ended up there, about our lives before prison, our fami-lies, and our current girlfriends. We also discussed the prison race wars and came to the conclusion that our fight had been necessary to prison and yard politics, which demanded that both of us represent our respective races. A biracial verbal altercation meant that everyone on the yard was going to ex-aggerate gossip, instigate, and ultimately use us as pawns in a bizarre chess game played out against the backdrop of idle time. If we hadn't fought, we would have sealed our respective fates of being labeled weak and thus placed ourselves in grave danger for the rest of our terms. Once we fought and went to the hole, however, the political paradigm was upheld. Everyone was thereby satisfied and ready to move on to the next drama of the week.

Sondra and I came out of the hole the same day and were both heroes to our races. We were "convicts." Although we had become friends, we were bound to keep that on the down-low. I had passed a new test.

Over the next two years, I become intimately familiar with doing hole time for infractions of one kind or another. One particular point of contention came up repeatedly—sunsets or, rather, being deprived of them. Sunsets were something precious, a big deal to me, something I would steal any chance I could get to see. Having lived in Arizona most of my life, I had been privileged during monsoon season to witness the most exquisite sunsets on the planet. Some literally took my breath away. It was rough losing those completely natural, free displays of magnificence, and my defiance on this issue resulted in my being sent to the hole three or four times. Officer Hatton or Valenzuela would announce across the yard on a megaphone "YARD CLOSED!!!!!" On more than one occasion, I resisted and declared, "No, and I'm not going in." Every time, my defiance resulted in the officer's' radioing for recruits and "four-pointing" me, which meant that four of them would tackle me, secure both my arms and legs, and then drag me to the hole. Fifteen days in isolation each time for refusing a direct order was a small price to pay for those glimmers at sunset.

Another of my visits to the hole happened after two of us were "caught" playing catch with turnips on the back dock of the kitchen. We were written up for horseplay and got five days.

***

Smoking pot in prison was easy. The yard was big enough that we could strategically position ourselves to see guards coming from any direction, leaving us time to eat the evidence. Usually we walked the track with the joint coupled in our hands. That was the best way. Snorting or shooting dope was pretty easy, too, if you had good pinners. The pinner's duties were to watch for the police and distract them from catching the group in any or all acts potentially punishable with hole time. Being a pinner was a serious designation; they were bound to protect the others at any cost, even by taking the rap themselves.

One day during my first year in, my home girls and I were hanging around in the yard, sharing a joint. Before smoking a joint, we would always determine who would hold the rest of the bag and who would pin. This time, I was given the job of holding the bag. This meant I could never let the officers get the dope. If push came to shove, I would eat what was left or put it down my pants. But on this day, the officers came fast, too fast for me to eat the evidence. So it went down my pants. They cuffed all of us and took us to the warden's office to be searched, but put me in a separate room. I had been schooled that even if you were holding, you could just refuse to be searched and go to the hole for refusing a direct order. This violation was worth only fifteen days in the hole, as opposed to thirty for possession and a drug charge on your jacket (prison file).

Lieutenant Giesenhoff, the associate warden, directed one of his officers to search me. When I refused, his face turned red and, clenching his bony, white fists, he punched me in the face. I was handcuffed to an office chair with wheels and tried to back away from him until I was up against a wall. He hit me again, barking, "Are you ready to be searched yet?"

"No way, you Gestapo prick," was my reply.

"Take her to the hole," he ordered Sergeant Craig.

And so I went, with my fifteen days, my black eye, and my pot. I guess Giesenhoff figured out that I would have taken more beating before I'd let him get the dope. But it was one of my best hole stints ever! That joint, plus the additional joints and matches that our dorm mates smuggled in to us under our toast, made this disciplinary action more like a party. It allowed all of us to laugh hysterically, philosophize about the meaning of life, and write flowery poems and letters. We used tampon wrapping to roll joints and lines to slide them to each other's cells. And when it was quiet and still, I let my own imagination soar the world over, to places I would, amazingly, see later in my life.

My experiences doing hole time sound colorful in the telling, but the reality is that thirty days of darkness, not knowing night from day, leaves one profoundly affected. The meals shoved through trap doors of our isolation cells were the only way of marking time. Cold oatmeal and dry toast were breakfast. Bologna, sometimes tinged green, meant it was lunchtime. Dinner was on a par with lunch, but even less exciting, consisting of a portion of what most convicts termed "mystery meat," cold, overcooked vegetables, and a slice of stale bread.

The hole—no sunlight, no moonlight. Graffiti lined the walls with silent death and suicide wishes, pledges of everlasting love, vows of regret, and pain. Roaches, crickets, and mice crept in, nearly sound-less but terrifyingly present. Those creatures became vivid monsters in hidden closets of my cell and my mind. Some made pets of them. I just couldn't.

CHAPTER 4
Angels and Fathers

Sometime around May 1975 (it just so happened I was in the hole, again), Sergeant Craig came to my cell around midnight, such an unlikely visit at that time of night.

"Looks like someone is getting a special visit tomorrow," she chirped, obviously enjoying my mystified look. She showed me a copy of a letter my mother had received from a private investigator in New York who had been hired by my biological father, Eddy, to locate me. He had only had my mother's maiden name to go by, because my mother had gotten their marriage annulled. He didn't even know my name.

I had never known my father. He was deported for bigamy when my mother was three weeks pregnant with me. According to my mother, he had told her to contact him if I was a boy, but not to bother if I wasn't. Clearly, she didn't. Throughout my childhood and while growing up with three stepfathers, my mother only told me three things about him. They were married atop the Empire State Building, he had worn a silk turban, and he kept a rock at the foot of their bed to ward off evil spirits.

Sergeant Craig went on to tell me my father would be there with my mother the next day, for a special visit approved by her because he had traveled from Germany. She almost seemed excited for me, but I was skeptical, stunned, and unable to sleep that night.

The day I met my father for the first time I was definitely not at my best after having spent the prior few weeks in the hole. Physically, since my arrival to prison, I had gained over ten pounds because of inactivity and the steady prison diet of starchy food. My face was seriously broken out. Mentally, I was disoriented and suffering the all-too-familiar consequences of spending more than twenty-five or thirty days in the hole.

31

That much time in isolation caused sounds, light, and voices to be distorted. Also, my bones ached as if I had a bad flu. It was hard to make complete sentences the first few hours out of the hole, and exposure to sunlight was excruciating.

My visitors arrived at noon, the brightest time of day. My vision blurred, I saw them sitting at a table. Because I had been in isolation, my security classification level had been elevated, and I was brought in shackled in waist and ankle chains. Both my mother's face and Eddy's reflected shock. It was my mother's first time visiting me in prison. She lived in Tucson, over 100 miles away, had little money, and my stepfather forbade her to see me. The three times she did visit she had to lie to him about where she was going.

My mother and I hugged. Over the next five hours, the three of us talked some, but mostly sat in awkward and uncomfortable silence.

I suspect Eddy was substantially disappointed at where he found me, with still over four years to serve. He tried not to show it. In halting English, he told me he was Italian like my mother, that he had grown up very poor, but had made a fortune for himself by playing bridge and exporting Mercedes Benzes and diamonds to America. Oddly enough, after all these years, there was no sign of tension between my parents, and the subject of why he had wanted to find me was never broached. He was a soft-spoken man with piercing hazel eyes. It was uncanny how much we resembled each other in our gestures and mannerisms. With his birthday just one day earlier than mine, we were both Aquarius.

He told me that when I paroled, I could come to Munich to work and help run the jeans shop he owned. Not only that, but ultimately, I would inherit part of his estate. The things he was saying and offering to me felt surreal, like something out of a movie. I wanted to believe him, but skepticism prevailed. I learned Eddy was married to a woman named Inga, but she had stayed back at their hotel room. He had taken a cab to my mother's house and they had driven two hours together to see me.

My father left $100 on my books and sent me this amount every month from then until the end of my term. I heavily suspected this was guilt money for the way he had left my mother and his unborn child twenty-two years earlier, but nevertheless it couldn't have come at a better time. To be without means in prison was potentially dangerous, and I certainly would have fared far worse than I did if not for that money. A hundred dollars a month was a fortune there.

My long-lost father was like an angel delivered into my life just when I needed one. I would meet him twice more, once two years later while I was still in prison and then six months after I paroled to the free world. The latter meeting would be our final one, because he passed away in 1982. His life and death, however, would later send me on a profound journey encompassing four countries and giving me experiences that, if they had not happened to me, I would not have imagined possible.

But for now, I still had over four years to serve.

Over the next couple of years, I spent a lot of time in the hole for infractions ranging from refusing to obey direct orders to possession of sugar. Sugar was deemed contraband because it was a key ingredient in making hooch. I was able to stay high each day probably four-and-a-half years out of my five flat. Never once did they get my drugs, nor find me dirty on urine testing. I was young and pissed off, so I rebelled. I remained with Judi, still feeling that "madly in love" part of being with someone.

It took two years for me to figure out the better way to beat the system was to make the officers believe I was conforming. You had to outsmart them, which fortunately proved not to be difficult at all.

CHAPTER 5
Moving to Durango

In 1978, Judi was called back to court on her appeal and won. They commuted her sentence to five years, four of which she had served. She would be leaving within weeks. It was so bittersweet. Now she would not have to leave prison in a coffin, but I still had two years. We vowed eternal love for each other before she left. She promised to wait for me, and we would live happily ever after once I was released.

In reality, Judi moved back to her hometown, San Luis Obispo, California, found a mountain man, and drank Jack Daniels and beer until she gained over 200 pounds. The first year I paroled, another home girl and I took a drive up the coast to see her. It was a strange visit and pretty unsettling to see her at 300 pounds when she had been so stunningly beautiful while we were together. Nevertheless, she lives on in that sacred place of my heart where other lovers do.

Not long after Judi paroled, the Men's Division rioted over crowded conditions, poor food, and negligent medical care. It was violent and highly publicized, and as a precautionary measure, the women were moved from where we were located, in a rural town called Florence, to one wing of a county jail called Durango in Phoenix. We were kept at Durango for nearly two years. Meanwhile, thousands of male prisoners were transferred to what had become our home, the Women's Division.

The public protested the move of a women's prison from Florence to Phoenix. An officer who worked at Folsom Prison in California wrote a letter to the editor of the *Phoenix Gazette*, asking not to be identified, in which he stated, "Prisoners are animals and if there is a prison break, and I pray there won't be, they'll do anything to stay out. What can be even worse is the quality of the people who visit the prisoners; you find that the visitors are sometimes worse than the convicts, and the guards are just a step away." He referred to the move as "horrifying."

By design, prisons and jails are constructed differently. Prisons are meant for long-term stays; jails are not. Prisons are for those who have already been tried, convicted, and sentenced; jails are for those who are pending all these and have significantly shorter terms than prison inmates. Because Durango was a jail, our lives as long-termers were dramatically affected. We no longer had yard time, jobs, or programs.

Our wing of Durango looked like a spider, the "body" of which was a huge dayroom. The legs of the spider were four housing pods that branched out, with thirty-two cells in each pod. In the dayroom, we could sit on metal benches bolted to the floor and watch small televisions secured high on the walls. In the center of this room was a control "bubble," similar to the red hourglass on the abdomen of a black widow. Encased in bulletproof glass, it looked out to the dayroom and the pods. From the bubble, armed officers could see everything and use the intercom's loudspeaker to yell out "COUNT," "CHOW," "MEDS," "YARD," and "MAIL." There was always something being barked over that loudspeaker. My guess was that some of those officers just liked to hear the sound of their own voices.

The most devastating consequence of the move to Durango was that our yard time was reduced from nearly eight hours per day to one. And frequently, we even lost that one hour if some issue arose, such as the silverware count in the kitchen coming up short. Everyone would be placed on lockdown until the missing fork, knife, or spoon was found.

The jail prisoners had priority treatment at this facility, because they were considered less dangerous than we were. For this reason, there were no jobs available to long-termers, as these were given to the jail prisoners. At Florence, we could make up to thirty cents an hour, good money then. Here, there were no jobs. I was lucky, though. The loss of my kitchen job pay at Florence was offset by my father's regular money orders.

We were kept in the pods, with limited access to the dayroom. By day, we were deemed trustworthy enough to use toilets at will and as needed. But at night, 10:00 to be exact, we suddenly became a security risk and were locked in our toilet-less cells until 6:00 a.m. One officer worked this shift, and when she wasn't asleep, she controlled unlocking the doors. Or not. We had to wave frantically out of our tiny windows and yell, or bang objects on the metal doors to our houses, in mostly vain attempts to get her attention. Usually we were left with only a waning hope that during this officer's rounds, she would stumble upon us, our bladders bursting, and unlock our houses so we could run to the toilet.

Needing to take a shit was more interesting. After learning the futility of trying to get the officer's attention, we devised makeshift toilets from small metal garbage cans lined with a tee shirt. Once released from our cells in the morning, we hand-washed the tee shirt to be used again the next night. It also helped to try training our bladders by not drinking any liquids after dinner.

This was Corrections at its best. I never again took for granted my freedom to pee.

When Judi left, I was suddenly elevated to "good catch" status within the prison community. I had established my name on the yard, had a lot of money on my books, and was without a partner. Almost instantly, Jackie—a tiny, pretty brunette with blue eyes who was also doing five flat—started flirting with me. Within a month we were a couple.

Unlike Judi, Jackie was insanely jealous and possessive, the first of only two lovers in my life to hit me. At the time, I thought her suspiciousness and fits of anger meant she loved me. And she took me to new heights of sexual experience, heights I had never known. She was such a seductive woman. Her passion, intensity, and rage took over my very being, whether she was beating or loving me. She was the best sex-ed teacher I ever had, but also the most violent partner. Many of my home girls told me I was stupid and weak to stay with her, and many times they threatened her on my behalf. I don't know how or why I stayed in the relationship for over a year. I suppose she gave me something I needed.

It wasn't too long before we all adjusted to Durango. We sometimes carried the ideals of fairness, justice, and logic as far as we could, but then had to get hold of ourselves and remember that prison, corrections, and doing time were a deck of cards stacked against us; the rules of play were often senseless. No yard, no programs, no work. Even so, it was fascinating to see how much could be accomplished with nothing but time. We always found ways to get high, make love, fight, and cook our four-course dinners with irons, popcorn poppers, and the like.

Our daily hour of yard time—if we were lucky enough to earn it, that is—was spent in the main yard. Here, we could walk a track about the length of a football field and get fresh air and direct sunlight. Also, attached to the back of each pod was a caged patio, six by six feet square and ten feet high. We had access to these all day, and we loved our patio cages. We sunbathed in them, grew vegetables in them (especially collard greens, which seem to grow anywhere), and could even see a "checkerboard" sky from inside them. To me, that was the best part.

***

Finally, the governor appointed a new warden from the Midwest do something about the lack of programs at Durango. Most wardens at that time were male, in their fifties, and good ol' boys. Warden Poole, a female, had been instrumental in getting Carol Fugate released in 1976 after she had served nineteen years. Carol Fugate was a girl from Nebraska who at fourteen years old and with the help of her boyfriend, Charlie Starkweather, had killed all of her family and seven others. The horrific and brutal murders had garnered worldwide attention, as did Warden Poole as a result of her subsequent involvement in the case. Arizona corrections had suffered negative publicity since the riots at Florence and was seen as archaic in their approach to rehabilitation. Warden Poole was young and progressive, a hoped-for solution to the issues of the widely criticized department.

While at Florence before Durango, I had earned a G.E.D. and an Associate Degree. Before that, my brain potential had all but ceased to develop when I began using drugs at age eleven. I had been an honor roll kid until then. Surprisingly, I discovered that doing time brought back my ability and passion for reading, writing, and learning. Here at Durango, however, there were few educational opportunities.

After exhausting the educational opportunities inside the walls after three years, I decided to ask this new, progressive warden if I could go outside trustee (OT) to Arizona State University in Tempe to pursue my Bachelor's Degree. She had already implemented other OT positions for inmates with good behavior, most of them low-paying jobs that fed the prison industries monster, which in turn lined the pockets of state officials. Prison industries are big money. The inmates of

Arizona prisons at that time made every license plate in the state for twenty-six cents an hour.

OT status was a sweet deal if you could get it. Until then, as far as I knew, no one had requested OT status to attend school, only to work. Another woman there, Mary, wanted to expand her education outside the walls, and so I wrote the proposal to the warden on behalf of both of us.

Upon summoning Mary and me to her office, she said, "If I allow this, you do realize it would be a first, right?"

"We do, and we know that means we have to do this thing right, and you have our word, we will," we replied.

Warden Poole looked at us, hard. "If you don't, trust me when I tell you, you will have hell to pay."

She granted both of us OT status to attend Arizona State University, a significant political gesture and leap of faith on her part. Indeed, it was a first in female corrections in Arizona.

What a trip! We were incognito, two convicts on a major state university campus. I was going to be a journalist. Mary majored in business. We both did well, but being good convicts, we used our new freedom to smuggle drugs into the prison, concealing them in our mouths or other body cavities. Between Mary and me, we knew many women who had paroled, and they bought us money and drugs two or three times a week.

Times were good for everyone. The yard and many of our home girls were rolling in money and dope because of our connections outside.

***

Like the new fish that had to endure a series of tests when they arrived at prison, fresh officers faced scrutiny from all of us as well. They had to prove themselves worthy of our distorted definition of respect. The difference in the case of officers, of course, was that if they didn't pass, they got to leave after eight hours to go to their homes and lives, not subject to the brutal repercussions we prisoners were. Nevertheless, it was easy for us to make their lives miserable during the time they were with us.

Career corrections officers often adopted the habits and attitudes of the convicts over their years of service. I often heard them refer to their seniority the same way the convicts referred to their sentences. It made me wonder what it took for someone to spend his or her life watching over prisoners, ensuring and contributing to the injustice, the violence, and the oppression.

Sergeant Singh was someone no one respected, liked, or tolerated. Even her fellow officers looked down on her. She was known for her tendency to abuse her power, probably her only recourse in light of the humiliation she suffered for failing to earn the respect she knew she didn't have and never would.

Three months into my OT studies at Arizona State, a home girl brought me a half ounce of pot. As always, I broke it up into smaller packages, wrapped them in rubbers, and keestered them. Upon returning to Durango, Sergeant Singh met me in the sally port, the main entryway into the prison complex with two gates, at the front and rear, used to enclose a person or vehicle. I knew something was up the instant I saw her, greasy-haired slob that she was, nearly as fat as she was tall. After searching my school backpack and patting me down, she said, "You're coming with me right now to see the nurse." She cuffed me and led me to the infirmary.

I knew she knew something, but had no idea what or how. Somebody had to have snitched. She told me I would stay with her until I shit or dug the pot out and turned it in. Yeah, right. The police were hip to keestering, so she told me if I didn't retrieve it for her, I would be forced to lie on a cold steel table and take an enema while she and the nurse observed me.

After not one, but six grueling and painful enemas, I still had my pot. Years earlier, I had used the same method to smuggle ounces of heroin and cocaine to the States from Mexico. I knew how to keep the dope inside me until such time that I wanted it out. And at this point, it wasn't coming out if she gave me sixty enemas. Sergeant Singh was defeated, for the moment anyway.

"I told you there was nothing there," I sneered at her.

Singh's barked commands through clenched teeth and trembling hands. Her sweaty face became increasingly red as her frustration mounted. We had been with the nurse for nearly three hours, and they were both on overtime. She took me to my cell, stripped it and me down, and rifled through all my clothes, bedding, books—basically anything that was my property—before letting me take a shower, which was the first minute I had away from her all day. I got the pot out, washed the rubber around it thoroughly, and had it cuffed in my hand as I came out of the shower. She didn't see it as she led me back to the dayroom. My hand relaxed as she started to leave me there, and unfortunately she caught sight of my prize. She ran toward me as fast as her fat ass could carry her. But not fast enough. Just as she was almost on me, I threw it across the dayroom into the crowd that had formed by then. Jackie grabbed it. Singh didn't know who had it, and she was beyond pissed. There was no way she would find it now, and she surrendered. I had won this battle.

Jackie stashed the pot in her cell. We all got high later that night and enjoyed hysterical laughter at Sergeant Singh's expense.

She still wrote me up for refusing a direct order. But even there in prison, we got due process, if one could call it that. When prisoners were accused of violating *Title 15*, the rulebook Sergeant Craig had given me my first day in prison, the officials had to formally serve us with a 115, similar to an indictment, and the 115 was heard in front of what we termed a "kangaroo court." This court was composed of the sergeant, a non-uniformed staff person such as a teacher or counselor, and one correctional officer. For some violations, such as assault, fighting, and attempted escape, the prisoner was sent immediately to the hole, and any arguments were heard later.

After my 115 was heard, I lost my OT status and went to the hole for the first time in over a year. The drag about hole time was that the prisoner lost two-for-one time credit, meaning she wound up serving more time. With my term of five flat, I would be eligible for parole, but only if I conformed.

Right then, though, conforming was not something I was ready to do.

Ultimately, Sergeant Singh got me back. The second time my father came from Germany to visit me, she was on duty and claimed she couldn't find the memo from the warden approving an extension of the length of my visit from one to five hours. After an hour, she sent him away for security reasons, she said. I hated her even more for that. She was one of two people in my life I could have hurt without remorse. I used to fantasize about what I would do to her and her family if I ever saw her on the streets. I know I wasn't the only one who thought that way about her.

After my 115, Warden Poole called me to her office for a reprimand. She had taken a great risk in allowing me OT status to go to Arizona State. My screwing up had made her look bad, and she was incensed, to say the least. Her words, spat at me with bitter disdain, are ones I will never forget: "You'll never make it out in the world. In here, you are a big fish in a little pond, but out there, you're a little fish in a big pond, and you can't handle that. In here, you are somebody. But out there you're not, and never will be."

Slowly, things at Durango improved. Warden Poole started bringing in programs and hired a chubby ex-Marine named Chuck as recreation director, a position unheard of before this. He was what they termed free staff, anyone working for the prison who wasn't a corrections officer.

Hired to establish a recreation program, Chuck had more latitude in treating us like people because he didn't work for corrections. Unlike many of the officers, who were cynical, angry, miserable, and uneducated, he had a natural enthusiasm and smiled often. A couple of us got jobs as his assistants. With his support and approval, we fought for and got more yard time, formal exercise sessions, baseball, volleyball, and a small monthly newspaper written by the inmates called *Feminine Focus*. Of course, the warden had to approve each issue.

Working on the newspaper became an outlet from the isolation of my cell and from Jackie, who by then was becoming increasingly violent and terrifying to me. We had a tiny office with two IBM Selectric typewriters. Writing took me beyond the prison and made my time go faster. Using it as a way to make sense of things, to bring order to the commotion in my head, I made my words fit into the airless space where I existed. I wrote about loving someone in prison, oppression, and the strangeness inside and around me. I wrote a monthly astrology column that warned of falling objects from the sky or predicted the great fortune of getting a letter every day. I wrote columns on how I saw the world outside that we prisoners weren't allowed to see. Newspapers and television news were forbidden to us, to prevent us according to the officers from getting any news that might provoke an escape attempt, such as someone we knew getting killed or dying. Even though we might eventually find out, their objective was to prevent an immediate or dramatic incident. When a death in an inmate's family did occur, she was summoned to a counselor's office and told in the presence of the prison chaplain. The prisoners were rarely allowed to attend the funerals of their loved ones.

I wrote one column for the prisoners on how not to let their time get them down. The byline was an old prison cliché, "Don't let your time do you." I wrote poems derived from my fantasies, memories, and imagination, poems about being twenty-four years old and caged, full of optimism some days and dying a thousand deaths on others. I wrote of days long gone, so I wouldn't forget the free world. I wrote wishes for the women I watched depart Durango from the front sally port. Almost every day, someone's time was up and she was transported in an old red pick-up truck, to work furlough, to the local Greyhound Bus Depot, and to a halfway house. Halfway to where I didn't know. But I did know someday it would be me leaving in that pick-up, headed halfway to something better.

Another extraordinary thing about working on the newspaper was that it allowed me to correspond with a national network of people who supported prison struggles, mostly prison activists, women's groups, and LGBT (lesbian, gay, bisexual, transgender) organizations. Tirelessly, I read what they sent me and I lived vicariously through them. The women's movement was in full swing throughout the 1970s. My first glimpse of the gay world outside prison was through literature. By the time I paroled, I took with me the five boxes of books, articles, and journals I had collected from those kind people at no charge.

Prison had become my life. It had to be for me to survive. Then it became so real that the world outside faded into a distant memory. The days were serious and our lives came down to smaller moments and things. We were making our histories in those miniscule houses, trying to gain a deeper understanding of what could not be seen, but only felt, remembered, or imagined. Reading, writing, music, pot, and love saved me. Saved my soul and mind.

***

My job assisting Chuck was very fulfilling. And even better, I once again found myself falling in love. I was still with Jackie, but it was bad. She was on OT status by then, driving prison-grown produce to local markets. Soon to parole, she was preoccupied with dreams of men and freedom, but not so much that she didn't still feel like she owned me. Jackie's feelings and actions toward me exemplified the old cliché "I don't want you, but no one else is going to have you either."

Enter Diana, who also worked for Chuck and with whom I spent several hours each week in the recreation office. We bonded quickly and tightly. It was clear to both of us that we had a nearly instant attraction. No doubt, the violence and jealousy in my relationship with Jackie made it that much easier to seek attention from Diana. Both of us began to dread Fridays because it meant we would be apart for two days. We longed to be together openly, but knew we had to bide our time until Jackie paroled.

On weekends, prisoners were sometimes allowed to watch movies while camped out on the dayroom floor with pillows and blankets. It was the best and easiest way for lovers to exchange hidden secrets of sex under the blankets, an intimate sort of slumber party. Eventually, the police figured it out, and after that we had to sit in metal folding chairs while watching movies. But even in those, after the movie began and the lights went out, the opportunity for sex was more than possible. Deprivation does breed ingenuity.

Physical contact of any kind with other prisoners was prohibited, a rule that seemed wholly unnatural to me, especially for us who were so young and were there for years on end with hormones raging. But the inability to have sexual intimacy was less devastating than being restricted from any contact whatsoever. Among the pile of literature I had collected, I learned of Dr. Renee Spitz. In the 1950s he studied the effects on World War II orphans of being denied human touch or nurturing, starting in infancy and sometimes continuing for years, because the orphanages were so overwhelmed with children. He filmed and wrote about these orphans, documenting that the babies had a very high rate of what was then called marasmus. Today, it is termed acute failure to thrive, or attachment disorder. Even though the orphanage was clean, and the babies were warm and dry, had adequate food, and all their other physical needs met, between thirty-five and forty percent of them wasted away and simply died. Dr. Spitz was determined to find the reasons for their deaths, as the children's environmental conditions seemed more than adequate and no physical diseases could be identified. He finally concluded that the cause of their deaths was not physical but related to emotional scarcity. One might say they died from broken hearts. Adults with these same symptoms are diagnosed with psychological and/or psychiatric disorders, both of which are rampant among the prison population.

Dr. Spitz confirmed his findings by hiring grandmothers to come into the nurseries to hold and cuddle the children, which resulted in rapid declines in the illness and mortality rates. Expanding on his findings, he wrote that from the time we are children, especially in America, we are actively discouraged from touching each other. Other studies have supported his early work. In prison, this "no touching" phenomenon is exacerbated, to the extreme of being a punishable offense. Nevertheless, we found ways to touch and to be touched in gentle, nurturing ways.

One Friday night, while lying there with Jackie and dreaming of Diana, I got up and went to the bathroom. There was Diana. I threw my arms around her and kissed her. Jackie walked in and saw us, pulled a pair of scissors from her back pocket, and lunged toward Diana. I immediately jumped between them and Jackie froze, stunned that I would let her stab me rather than Diana. She left the bathroom defeated, knowing whatever had existed between us was over and that no matter how many times she screamed at me or beat me, it wouldn't matter.

Diana and I were together from that night until I paroled. She changed me profoundly and forever.

CHAPTER 6
Furlough

A few months after I lost OT status, Warden Poole distributed a memo stating that anyone with less than two years left to serve could request a 72-hour furlough. Apparently, this had always been the case, but none of us had heard of it. It was a well-kept secret that, once leaked, started a frenzy of approved furlough requests. To ask for and actually be permitted three days in the free world was too good to believe!

By this time, I had been without a 115 for over six months and was back in good graces with the administration. I was still scamming, scheming, using dope, and continuing my efforts to break every rule I could, but in the eyes of the administration, I was a good convict who had not caused any problems for a while. I applied for and received a furlough.

I was approved to go to Tucson, the home of my mother, Stephanie; brothers, Nate and Jonathan; and sister, Jeanette. My mother and Jeanette had only been able to visit me twice in prison. Nate had never visited, and Jonathan had come once, a couple years earlier.

When Jonathan had visited, I revealed to him I was gay and told him about Judi, whom I was with at the time. I was certain that she and I were going to be together forever, so why shouldn't I tell him about her? Of anyone in my family, I figured he would be the most open to my new lifestyle. This was my first experience with coming out to anyone outside prison.

Jonathan seemed okay with it when I told him, but as it turned out, it seemed he might not have been. He never explicitly told me his true feelings about it, but they certainly became clear during my furlough in Tucson.

After spending the first day with my mother and Jeanette, I left that night and went to Jonathan's. While I had been away, I discovered he had found new lifestyles and interests, including becoming a full-fledged cowboy who rode in rodeos, roped cattle, and raised horses. He also identified himself as a card-carrying member of a motorcycle club, an offshoot of the Hell's Angels called The Huns. He lived in a double-wide trailer with his girlfriend, Alana, on the outskirts of Tucson at the foot of the Saguaro National Monument, a park on Tucson's west side where thousands of saguaro cacti stand tall and reach for the sky like a legion of soldiers in the desert. Their trailer was also not far from Gates Pass, a breathtaking valley in the middle of the monument, where we had partied together all throughout the 1960s. In this breathtaking place, we had taken acid trips, gotten drunk, and smoked pot under the brightest stars I've ever seen, with a full moon illuminating the whole mountain.

Jonathan said to me, "C'mon with us to a party. I've got a friend I want you to meet. He's bringing his bike over and you can ride with him."

His friend's name was Johnny, a skinny, gray-bearded biker who looked to be around forty. I was excited. I hadn't been on a Harley in years. When we arrived at Gates Pass, they had dug a pit and were cooking a goat on a skewer fashioned out of mesquite branches. They had a keg of beer, hard liquor, speed, and a lot of pot. The men were all sitting around the fire drinking, and the women were huddled in another group talking. Kids were running around playing, between taking sips of beer and hits off joints. Even though I had ample drugs in prison, when I got high there, I had to maintain a low profile to avoid being caught. But this occasion was like old times, partying without having to hide it!

By two in the morning, I was so loaded that I became anxious and started getting paranoid. I hadn't been this high in years. I wanted to leave and started looking for Jonathan to tell him, but he was gone. I couldn't believe he'd left me stranded and not knowing how I was going to get back to his house. Fortunately, I found Johnny and asked him if he would take me back to Jonathan's. Grumbling, he agreed to it. Amazingly, even though we were both fucked up, his driving wasn't affected one bit. It felt awesome to be soaring out Ajo Way on his Harley.

When we got to Jonathan's house, though, I discovered I was locked out. With this turn of events came the sudden realization that he may have set this whole thing up. It should have been obvious to me that the cultures of bikers and cowboys wouldn't be tolerant of my gayness, plus it was still the late 1970s, decades before being gay was even a little bit accepted. Sadly, we're still fighting for acceptance as part of mainstream society. I'll never know whether Jonathan arranged this situation to give me no other choice than to be with this guy Johnny in the middle of the night. Johnny didn't live far away, and I think he was as uncomfortable as I was about the whole situation. He offered to let me sleep on his couch and bring me back the next morning. I agreed to it, but first we went out to Denny's for breakfast, one of those great, after-getting-drunk-and-high breakfasts that taste so amazingly good. By then it was nearly dawn.

Once at his place, Johnny started making out with me. Because I had come out in prison and wasn't completely sure about my sexual identity, I decided to go with it, have sex with him just to see if I still liked men. I hadn't been with a man in over five years, and my last time had been a brutal and violent encounter. But sex with Johnny felt awkward, gruff, and scary. The further we went, the more I knew that I no longer wanted to be with men.

Finally, I stopped him and said, "Uh-uh, I can't go through with this. I'm so sorry." I was truly embarrassed and felt bad for him.

"Aw, come on, I think you can," he replied, continuing to kiss me.

When I couldn't or wouldn't return his kiss, he stopped, to my relief and surprise. We slept for a few hours and then he took me back to Jonathan's.

My brother and I have never spoken of that night since, but many years later, he was one of two best men at my wedding to a woman.

I spent the next day and a half with my mother, and she drove me back to Durango on Sunday. Going back after the furlough to finish my two years was nothing to me. By this time, I realized I had grown quite comfortable in prison and couldn't wait to get back to my girl.

CHAPTER 7
Armantha

If ever in my life I have met evil up close, it was in the form of a woman named Armantha, a lifer who had done nine years when I first met her. Armantha shot her boyfriend's lover in cold blood in front of the woman's mother and children. Afterward, she kept the bullet casings and showed them off around the poor, south-side Tucson neighborhood where she lived, with full knowledge she would be picked up and sent to prison. She didn't care. She was proud of her feat and sick enough to flaunt it in front of anyone unfortunate enough to know her.

Armantha controlled everyone at Durango, including the warden and officers, through sheer intimidation. The fact that her health was failing, as evidenced by her diabetes and the difficulty she had just walking, cemented the impression that she had nothing left to lose. Out of fear, nobody wanted to anger her, even though she was a blatant, outright snitch. The only option within our prison community was to try to stay in her good graces, meaning that if she ordered you to do something, you did it without question or hesitation.

One time, during my first year in prison, she had asked me to watch a crock-pot full of pinto beans she was cooking, and I completely forgot about them and let them burn. The next day I was in the hole for a rig (syringe) that mysteriously turned up in my house during the surprise search the night before.

Another time, around Christmas during my first or second year, Judi had screwed one of the men (not her husband, Mark, but some gaunt, old, toothless guy who looked old enough to be her father) in my dorm while others pinned for her. She claimed it was for money, which he did give her, but part of me knew she missed sleeping with men. Sick with embarrassment and humiliation, I decided to check myself into the hole to save face.

My plan backfired thanks to Armantha, whom I had learned by then to keep on good terms.

"Sergeant Craig, if Denise's goin' to the hole, I'm goin' too. She ain't goin' to be in der alone," Armantha said, for some reason I couldn't even begin to fathom.

"Damn, Armantha! C'mon, just let me go and get some space," I pleaded.

"If you're goin', I'm goin' too," Armantha retorted, planting herself firmly next to the door.

"Armantha, you know I won't take you to the hole with me on Christmas, YOU KNOW THAT! That's why you're doin' this," I yelled.

"Den I guess you ain't goin'," she cackled.

It was one of the rare times I saw her show any shred of empathy, or was it; who knows? So I opted not to go to the hole. As humiliated as I felt, the prospect of spending even one day in the hole with Armantha, and the fear that I would pay a price at some future point, or at least be indebted to her, was worse.

Armantha had several special privileges. Most of us were not allowed to have unapproved food in our houses. Approved food was limited to what one could buy from the commissary, with the exception of the few weeks around Christmas. At that time, each of us was allowed one box of goodies from our family (the box could weigh no more than twenty-five pounds). These boxes were filled with home-cooked, delectable chocolate chip cookies, brownies with and without pot, banana, zucchini, and cranberry bread, and more. We feasted at Christmas, one of the, if not THE, highlights of each year. But not Armantha, who feasted year round. Her house was like a Jewish or Italian deli. Even more remarkable, though, was that it was often the officers who smuggled these delicacies to her. It was said that the warden once brought her a rare French cheese. Armantha was an accomplished manipulator who always got her way using an arsenal of intimidation, threats, and the like. She used her age and various physical afflictions to garner support and sympathy from both inmates and staff. For many years, it worked.

***

Reading, writing, and working on *Feminine Focus* made me feel as though I was growing wings. I had been lucky because neither Chuck nor even Warden Poole censored the majority of the articles I wrote. But now, I was taking a chance by turning in final copy about a particularly horrific episode involving Armantha, who had committed an act of such malicious cruelty that the subsequent lack of punishment for it infuriated me.

"I'm not even going to submit this to the warden," Chuck said after looking it over. "You know you can't attack the administration."

"Why the hell not, Chuck? Do you think I'm right?" I asked.

"You know I do," he replied. "But that's not the point."

"It doesn't say her name," I persisted. By this time I was screaming at him.

"Dammit, Denise, you know if this gets printed, everyone on the yard knows what happened. Everyone will know it was her!"

"What about the paper being by the inmates, for the inmates, Chuck? What about that!" I yelled.

"The subject is closed. It's not going in, period!" he said, in a tone that precluded further discussion. But it wasn't closed for me. I went on, as I stomped out of the office, "Hey Chuck, you know all your great speeches about being fair? Put 'em where the sun don't shine! Screw you."

Chuck and I argued often and passionately. He could have written me up many times for insubordination, but didn't. On this particular occasion, I left work knowing I needed to cool off. I also knew that when I saw him later, we would carry on as if nothing had happened. I churned over and over in my mind Chuck's reasons for not printing the article. I thought it was the most important thing I had written. After years of numbness to the violence around me, I thought nothing could shock me anymore. But Armantha had managed to break through my thick and carefully laid walls, and devastated, I had poured out my agony, the injustice of it all, and most important, the opinion of nearly every woman on that yard. We needed to be heard.

A few convicts, headed by a woman named Andy, got stoned one day and got brave so they plotted and stole a bag of potato chips from Armantha's house. Days passed after the theft, and nothing happened. Perhaps she hadn't noticed. But soon enough, we found out she had. It was one of those terrifying Armantha transformations from calm to beyond evil. When she discovered her house had been burglarized, her black skin flushed crimson, enough to make her coloring go a shade of orangish-brown, and her eyes shone bright and crazy with hatred and vengeance.

When Armantha was going to strike, she usually didn't do it right away. She lived for the build-up of fear and tension she created. She waited.

Then the day came. She filled a thirty-six-cup coffee pot with water, boiled it steaming hot, and added bleach. With her best-trained henchwomen posted to pin (settling this score would only take seconds), she hobbled across the dayroom carrying the coffee pot, her aged, decrepit body burdened with the weight of that water. Small groups of women stood here and there watching in helpless horror.

When she reached her prey, she uttered, "Andy, turn roun' so I kin see you."

Andy's eyes met Armantha's and were assaulted by the venomous water, which crashed like a wave onto her face and then washed over her chest and legs.

Andy was sightless and speechless. Her girlfriend Karla ran frantically to find the guards. Within minutes, even the concrete seemed to know what had happened. The roar of malevolence gave way to stunned silence all over the prison.

Andy was rushed to the county hospital, treated, and bandaged from her face and neck down to her knees, all while Armantha sat in her house, eating and reveling in satisfaction of a job well done. Her victim would scar severely, but fortunately not lose her eyesight. Sharon, a fellow prisoner and renowned jailhouse lawyer who had spent a good portion of her prison time helping other inmates with appeals and writs, offered to file a lawsuit for Andy against the state regarding their decision not to charge Armantha with assault. Sharon was as brilliant as any lawyer on the streets and was paroling that week. Unfortunately, though, once she paroled, she was never heard from again and never filed the lawsuit for Andy.

Years after I paroled, I heard they moved Armantha to a maximum-security prison in Texas after she attempted to stab an associate warden with a pair of scissors.

Witnessing all of this destroyed any shred of belief in justice I had managed to cling to. It felt as though in one year at Durango I had heard the song of life and death a million times, but a million was practically none compared to infinity. Barely arm's length from this new vision of cruelty, I placed myself in a bubble where I could walk, talk, even sleep, with my thoughts detached and wandering in and out of prison. Forced to accept this fate of helpless frustration about the absurdity of life there, I had to keep fighting. For what, I wasn't sure.

CHAPTER 8
Short Time

Perhaps it was illusion, or love, or both that made my life in prison go on, at times even blissfully, with Diana. I was spellbound in love. A wounded, brilliant woman who had spent much of her life in either foster homes or institutions, Diana was extremely well-read and held an endless store of information about art, music, literature, politics, and more—everything it seemed to me. Learning from her and with her was strange, wondrous, and magical. We shared our secrets, fantasies, schemes, ideas, and deep love. I hated spending one minute away from her. With Diana, empty spaces inside me that I hadn't even known existed were filled, taking me to some sort of wholeness I had never experienced.

The years she had spent in tiny cells forced Diana to create an imaginary life, one she could almost see. And through her, this life became real to me also. I learned from her how to care about things I'd never thought about: war, oppression, the universe. She taught me cynicism and even rage at the system she convinced me had put us both in prison. And so much poetry! I learned poems from her and composed poems about her. Every day we wrote each other pages filled with longing, using words picked out of lonely nights because we lived in different pods and could only spend the days together. Just thinking about her made me feel as though I was breaking through closed doors. Visions would come to me of going to the mountains with her, living with her there, basking in the abundance of a green spring and then being quietly humbled by winter's snow, or seeing an ocean. Sometimes, though, a deep and untouchable sadness came over her, reflected in her eyes, which suddenly appeared hollow, ancient, and tired. They weren't at all the eyes of a woman only twenty-five years old.

But even the enchantment of my love for Diana couldn't prevent those last two years of prison from taking a heavy toll on me. It grew harder and harder to write my mother and tell her I was okay. I wasn't. As much as I tried to maintain a stance of indifference to the politics, the cruelty, the games, and the violence around me, I could not. I went to a cold, black, and pitiful place where I was at the mercy of my anguish about where and who I was. Here, my fantasies turned inside out and became disillusionment.

Ironically, though, I feared the notion of ever leaving. In prison, having only a year left is considered short if you've already done four or five. Like everyone I had watched before me, I was packing up and sending boxes home so I wouldn't have as much to take out when I paroled. I continued to work for Chuck and managed to stay out of the hole. My articles were as radical as they would let me print. Writing was my catharsis, my release, the jumbled emotions within me cascaded onto paper. If surviving here meant giving up my body and soul, I still had my mind if I could write. Our little prison newspaper, *Feminine Focus*, even had a mailing list of over fifty people in the free world.

Warden Poole moved on, and another warden came and went. Over my five years in state prison, the Women's Division went through five Department of Corrections directors, three governors, and eleven wardens of the women's prison. All, of course, had different ideas about the meaning of rehabilitation and/or punishment. Every time the administration changed so did the rules, including the censorship rules for the paper. While forcing smiles at the correctional staff, I wrote about them. I referred to them as enemies with badges, scum who ruled us, tyrants who caused already frail people to go mad. Most of those words didn't make the paper.

I also wrote articles directed at the convicts, whom I scolded for their continuing instigation, racism, and pecking-order politics. I couldn't understand how they, so oppressed themselves, could justify oppressing each other. How dare they? How could they live with themselves? But over and over, this senseless behavior—overwhelming hatred among people during the Holocaust, in the Middle East, in prisons everywhere, among gang members, within families, people railing against each other—has occurred throughout history and continues today. Such behavior is a human phenomenon I have yet to understand, but it fills me with confusion, disillusionment, and, back then, rage.

***

Five months before I paroled, they finally moved us from Durango into an old, run-down, abandoned former hotel on Thirty-Second off Van Buren Street called the Arizona Center for Women. The building and grounds were to be renovated just for us. A hotel. Really? We were floored. Because Diana and I were both short, we were chosen to be among the select few to go to the new prison and assist in getting it ready. Our jobs consisted of heavy yard work, clean up, and maintenance. It was hard physical labor, but as any convict would tell you, we loved physical work. Strenuous labor not only worked off pent-up frustration and anxiety, but also helped us stay in shape. To the delight of those from the Women's Division who were into men, male convicts from Florence were also brought in to help with the renovation.

At first, there were no walls or fences around the huge site, which covered acres and acres. We couldn't believe they were calling this a prison, soon to be populated with over 200 female convicts. It took two months for the work to be completed, during which time all of us took full advantage of the wide-open space and minimal supervision by officers. During our breaks, we had sex, got high and drunk, and generally whooped it up. It was almost like being free.

Then came the move. Diana and I were assigned to the same "cell," an actual hotel room with two queen beds, a dresser, and our own bathroom! It was heaven. Over the next few weeks, we had plants, music, food, friends, drugs, alcohol, and each other. We set up house.

The first day after everyone transferred was bizarre and comical— it just seemed too good to be true. Because of the size of the place, the officers had a tough time even counting us, which greatly pissed them off. For the first time in a long time, they couldn't see and hear everything from safe and convenient control bubbles. Speechless, we watched in awe through real glass windows, the officers trying to adjust to having little to no control over us. It was like a really good acid trip. Too bad I only had a few months left to serve. I really thought that. Sad but true.

Diana was supposed to get out five months after me, and I couldn't wait for our life to start in the free world. By then, I had many home girls who had paroled and were, as they had promised, taking care of Diana and me by sending us heroin, speed, and pot in packages. There were so many creative ways to get drugs through the mailroom. We were allowed hygiene items, and those on the outside could empty out a baby powder container, put in an ounce of pot or a few grams of heroin or speed wrapped in rubber balloons, and then cover it over with the powder. During the Christmas season, when we got those food packages, friends on the outside could smuggle drugs to us inside boxes of crackers, bags of cookies, etc. The mailroom officers randomly checked incoming mail, but generally only about five percent of it ended up being screened.

One of our home girls, Brenda, was married to a Japanese guy named Yutaka. Notorious in prison and on the streets for cooking methamphetamine, he was definitely someone you did not cross. He and Brenda had beautiful matching Harleys that Brenda sent us pictures of. Brenda was also sending us a lot of speed. We tweaked for weeks on end, shooting speed and then heroin to come down with. We loved the new expansive acreage we had to run and play in, before retreating to our little love castle where we took real bubble baths (for four years, I had not seen a bathtub), listened to music, wrote, read, and made love. Life couldn't have been better. I felt as though I could have stayed there with Diana like that forever.

And yet, I was so tired.

***

The morning began routinely enough. We were rousted out of bed in the usual rude and loud manner, with "BREAKFAST" blared over the loudspeaker. All meals were mandatory at this new prison and we had to be escorted back and forth to the chow hall, presumably for better control. After a brisk walk in the cool morning mist to the dining room and then lining up for cold waffles on which butter refused to melt, we just drank some coffee and asked to go back to our house. It had begun to rain, and Sergeant Singh was escorting us cattle style, looking more and more like an enormous, floppy whale as the rain drenched her huge body. Suddenly, she snatched Diana and me out of the line and whisked us off to the Security Control Office, where she ordered us to sit quietly and wait. Mystified, we asked another officer what was going on, but he told us to sit, keep quiet, and wait until the "fat lady" came back. He actually called her that.

When Sergeant Singh returned, she grabbed another officer and headed with him to our house, while Diana and I, still groggy with sleep, trailed behind. She fumbled with the lock for several minutes when she reached our house, so we finally opened the door for her. Once inside, she made straight for the bathroom—focused, surefooted, and determined—to where a spider plant nurturing a baby pot plant in the same pot hung in stillness in front of the tiny window. She snatched the plant, declaring dramatically that she was confiscating it. Diana and I had to bite our lips to keep from laughing out loud. All of this hysteria over a baby pot plant?

Sergeant Singh informed us she was writing us up and then commanded us to leave and get to work. "Your 115s will be processed and served later," she informed us. After getting ready for work in our house, we returned to the Control Office to obtain our written passes to the recreation office. On this second trip to Control that morning, we discovered that the fat lady had been busy. She sat at a desk eating and looking very smug and satisfied. Surrounding her were six or seven other baby plants that had been confiscated from various houses.

Immediately, we saw how easy it would be to rescue the sprouts. Within an hour, a few of us managed to get all the baby shoots out of Control, back to our houses, and placed in water-soaked paper until we found their rightful owners. Sergeant Singh's evidence for the 115s was gone. When she found out, she looked like she was about to have a heart attack, screaming at the two guards who let the plants slip right out from under them. How disappointed she must have been. All that great investigative police work for nothing.

With the evidence gone, we knew they had no reason to keep our spider plant, so we asked for it back. We were told they were keeping it for thirty days for observation. What? No way were they going to kill our plant! We waited until mail call, stole it back, and hid it in another room to ensure its safety from greasy, fat kidnappers. Within a few hours, we managed to get all the other plants out, too. Later that day, Singh came running out of the

Control Office, screaming once again and demanding the plants back. We told her we had no idea what she was talking about, and if our plant was gone, it was her fault!

It was final payback for the enemas and for cutting my father's visit short. Revenge felt sweet indeed.

CHAPTER 9
Parole

The closer I got to parole, the more confused my emotions, an unsettling mixture of excitement, intense sadness, and heart-pounding fear. Prison had grown on me, and most of the time I didn't mind it too much, yet I had always dreamed of and longed for the day I would leave. At one point, Diana asked me to get a 115 intentionally so I could extend my time, allowing us to parole closer to the same time. But even though I loved her intensely, it was too much to ask. I couldn't, just couldn't, stay a day longer than I had to. For nearly five long years, I had watched hundreds of women come and go. Some left on work furloughs, others in that red pick-up truck to halfway houses, and many into the welcoming arms of families, boyfriends, pimps, or girlfriends.

My soul was wounded and my dreams were dented. I felt the empty weight of this continually, except when I was with Diana. She still could take my breath away. Just looking at her made the days worth the trouble it was to wake up. She alone could give me those rare moments of joy, when my heart danced as she gazed at me with those smiling, bright eyes in the night, her fingers softly brushing over my eyelashes, my face, my neck, my breasts. Yes, with Diana my world was bearable.

But also in the night, I would listen to the songs rising out of the penitentiary darkness, someone's FM radio. In those moments, the silhouettes of tree branches outside the window seemed suddenly sad for the world. In those moments, I knew I was lost, a stranger to the wind that whirled around me, a stranger to myself. Desperately, I sought the comfort of connection, grabbing for sex, music, literature, Diana, and love. But it all became mixed up, and it mixed her up. In the hours after the sun fell, my mind was screaming to her, but I couldn't find words for the thoughts that kept me awake as I lay in my bed. Silently, I would grow downward, inch-by-inch, into childhood, but I still couldn't find my tears. Feeling as weak as a storm-wrenched leaf, my eyes aching from unshed rivers, I would forget that Diana and I dreamed our own seasons. So again I silently pleaded, please, just touch me! She would look at me strangely and say, "Tired?" Thank you. I had my moods, my piles, and my lists of things waiting to be done. But the closer to parole I came, the more the things I did that excluded her.

My plans beyond prison were to work and go to school, but most of all to cop some dope and do a speedball as soon as I could. I had earned a G.E.D. and Associate Degree and had applied to and been accepted at the University of Arizona in the Bachelor's program. To help finance my education, I had applied for grants and a student loan.

Also while inside, I had maintained contact with the drug program I was in before I went to prison, called Casa de Vida, or House of Life. Frank, an Italian dope fiend from Brooklyn turned Program Manager, had kept in touch with me more than anyone else, besides my new-found father and my mother. Every year he made sure that a Christmas box of goodies was sent to me, a gesture I never forgot. After release, I was going to the program for immediate shelter. I didn't want to live at home again even though my mother had long since left my stepfather and had offered me that option. I thought I should stand on my own two feet, though I had no idea what that meant outside the realm of crime and addiction.

From talking to others, I knew to expect that I would be dropped off at a Greyhound bus station in downtown Phoenix. I was told they would give me $50 gate or kick-out money, as it was called. I could take my few small boxes of mostly nothing: cherished books I had collected while working for Chuck, music, volumes of love letters, some scant clothing and hygiene items, and the three plants I had nurtured from cuttings.

I had been in the presence of only women until the last six months when the Department of Corrections, in their infinite wisdom, assigned male officers to female institutions, and vice versa. It made my last few months in prison entertaining, disgusting, and in some ways typical in terms of what happens when women broken, beaten, powerless, and oppressed are in situations with men who hold power. Male officers traded drugs, cigarettes, and money for sexual favors from the prisoners, convinced they had ultimate control and power. But in reality, the female prisoners used their own power and the situation to threaten, blackmail, and demand more drugs and money from them. One of my home girls seduced and got pregnant by an officer and then claimed she had been raped and sued the Department of Corrections. Unfortunately, after years in and out of prison, she died of a heroin overdose at only twenty-seven years old, after spending the $350,000 she had won in that lawsuit. I have known hundreds of men and women who traded sex for what they wanted or needed. The way I saw it, it was honest work in the sense that all parties knew why they were doing it and what they wanted out of it.

***

The night before I paroled, I dreamed of turkey baster binkies, which were crude homemade syringes constructed with used eyedroppers and old needles. The giant binky points were filled with ounces of uncured opium. Each time I stuck it in my arm, got a register, and oozed a few blobs, I'd get the uncontrollable urge to peck the ground and make gobbling noises. No matter how much I'd get in my vein, the effect was the same. I never got high and couldn't overdose, but I finally grew huge, heavy feathers that made my legs ache so much that it almost woke me up. Then, still half-asleep, I had fitful, dream-like visions of falling into an abyss of fire. Finally, my eyes opened completely, and I was soaked in sweat among twisted sheets. It was terrifying and I knew later a premonition of what would come, when heroin would become "my life, my wife," as the Lou Reed song "Heroin" so aptly said.

***

On February 28, 1980, I was sitting in a holding cell at 3:00 a.m., waiting while they processed my release paperwork. I had been there for hours, my mind wandering. I couldn't get rid of the nagging thought that my plants were dying. They had put my property somewhere else, and I had no control over how it was being handled. I torturously envisioned each leaf turning dull and limp, almost tasting the dry dirt and wishing I had tears to pour into their parched pores. Please, not so much sun, they begged, for they, like me, were used to artificial light. Don't touch them; they like to be alone. Just feed them, hope they grow, and if not, let them rot, I thought.

Occasionally, an officer checked on me, but mostly I was alone with my thousand thoughts, one for each beat of my heart. I felt as though I was groping for words that were just below the surface, swelling under my eyelids or deep inside the holes of my needle-pierced arms (from all the speed and heroin Diana and I had been doing those last few months). As the sun rose, feelings came and went like wild surf breaking against the reef. The tightness of my bra was killing me, and I could no more dismiss that annoyance than I could the pangs of anxiety about my impending freedom. In the next moment, I raged inside against all those who had condemned me for so long, assuring myself I had the right.

Damn, it was so cold in the cell! With no idea how long the processing would take, I asked them to turn on the heat. I tried to sleep, to let warm unconsciousness dispel the chill of my tired bones. I dozed and dreamed, but the dreams were harsh, turning the pure clouds of my illusions into gray storms of past and present ugliness. I woke up, startled, my mind in siege against the restraints of their cell, their prison, their walls, their razor wire. I imagined that the future they would predict for me would become their own death sentences, a reflection of the unhappy prisons they had built. *Dragnet* was theirs. I just wanted *Alice in Wonderland* back.

Five years in and, now, nearly out. I hoped that I still had a little laughter hidden safely in a remote corner of myself. I had cooked, and wept, and loved, and written in prison. I had earned twenty-six cents an hour, good money then. I had survived, and did not survive. My skin no longer fit my face, and talking and dreaming had somehow become entangled with my feelings. My mouth and eyes had been open most of the time, but I couldn't remember what I had said or seen. I did the five years the judge gave me, but I didn't know what I was supposed to do now instead of time, especially without Diana. My journal entry that day read, "Released from prison, February 28, 1980. #34749. Time served from September 24, 1975. About 2:00 p.m., 100 degrees outside."

The move shocked my plants.

PART TWO

BEFORE

CHAPTER 10
Stevie

1953. February. New York Hospital, New York. My mother, Stephanie, was twenty-three, unwed, and a strict Catholic when I was born on February 12, 1953. She rarely spoke about my father, Eddy, but when she did it was with fondness. Then again, I never heard her speak ill of anyone. Without exception, my mother was the most tolerant, patient, and unassuming person I've ever known. She always took life lightly, sometimes to a fault, and unfortunately this was the case in her choice of men, some of whom brought violence and harm down upon my two brothers, my sister, and me.

I am the oldest of four siblings, a product of my mother's first husband, Eddy. Her second was Jeff, the father of my two brothers, Jonathan and Nate. After this was Harvey—there were no children from that marriage—and finally Manny, father of my sister, Jeanette. I grew up never having met my father. He had been deported for bigamy when my mother was three weeks pregnant with me, never to be heard from again until I was twenty-one.

Now that I'm sixty and beyond, I understand, am grateful for, and cherish my mother. I didn't always. More than anything else, my mother taught me humility and tolerance. She was profoundly grateful for so little. Years of therapy helped me explore, sort out, and try to comprehend her life: her choices and mistakes, how they affected me, the ways I punished her, and how I eventually forgave her. I didn't volunteer for this therapy, but it was necessary for me to overcome a twenty-two-year drug habit and face the accompanying self-destructive and despicable acts on my part—all of them—in glaring and gruesome detail.

During one therapy stint, I asked my mother to write her story for me. She did so, and it was obviously a labor of love for her because she produced several honest, deeply touching pages that told of her life's journey. Reading it, I realized how important it was in helping me start to appreciate the biggest gift she had given me—life, as well as a mother I wouldn't have traded for any other.

My mother was born in June 1928 in a fourteen-room house that her father had built in Woodside on Long Island. Her parents had immigrated to New York from Naples, Italy. She and her identical twin, Eleanor, were so premature and tiny that my grandmother put them in a shoebox in the oven to incubate them. After that, they slept inside a dresser drawer.

By the time she and Eleanor (or Ellie, as she was affectionately called. My mother was Stevie, short for Stephanie) came along, many of their older siblings had died, my grandmother had told her. Most had passed at one or two years of age from childhood diseases such as whooping cough and diphtheria, diseases for which vaccines had not yet been developed. One of her brothers died of spinal meningitis at age nine. Another brother passed away from tuberculosis at age twenty-eight in a sanitarium in Utica, where he had lived for years. My mother couldn't forget my grandmother's screams when the hospital called to tell her of his passing. Before my grandmother died, she had lost nine children. My mother marveled at my grandmother's strength and said she was "the sweetest, most wonderful mother she could have ever asked for."

My mother and Ellie were the youngest of fourteen. My mother, like her mother, spent most of her life silent, suffering, and doing what she believed she was supposed to do. It was a time when *Better Homes and Gardens* praised First Lady Mamie Eisenhower for "not attempting to become an intellectual" and glowingly depicted her as a woman who was "no bluestocking feminist." In part, this was a backlash against the appointment of playwright Claire Booth as Ambassador to Italy in March of that year, the first woman to represent the United States in a major diplomatic office. Also, Eleanor Roosevelt publicly allied herself with the National Federation of Business and Professional Women. In the meantime, sixty-eight percent of all American televisions tuned in to watch Lucy give birth to Little Ricky, and Elvis made his first recording.

My mother described my grandfather as very strict and violent. He treated my grandmother like a doormat, calling her names and hitting her. He was a typical old-school Italian husband and father who ruled the roost, oftentimes with his fists. Even so, my mother described her childhood as beautiful and idyllic. In addition to school and studying, they always had a lot of work to do around the house.

Throughout her childhood, she remembered music the most. They had two pianos, one in the basement and one in the living room. Several of her brothers and sisters played instruments. Even after everyone was grown, they would all get together. My mother described these as occasions of great gaiety when the family cooked, sang, drank wine, and danced. This was during Prohibition, and her father was bootlegging. He had a still in the basement, and he and her mother went to jail more than once when the house was raided. Her father and uncles played bocce during clam parties under the grape arbor. The family went to the beach, to New York shows, and to Utica to see her Uncle Frank in the sanitarium. My mother and Ellie were very fond of Uncle Frank.

When Stevie and Ellie were thirteen, they went to St. Mary's parochial elementary school. At sixteen, they took a cooperative course in high school that provided them both with papers so they could work one week and attend school the other. They were "page girls" at Chemical Bank in Manhattan, earning $16 per week. Their salary covered all their expenses, plus paid their parents' room and board, unheard of in these days and times. My mother worked from then on. "Life went along," is how she put it.

Various siblings got married, and she and Ellie excelled at both work and school. They dated and used their identical appearance to sometimes switch dates, as well as classes at school. No one was the wiser. One memory my mother recalled was when her father didn't like one of her boyfriends and chased him down the street wielding an ax. Needless to say, boys were ever after afraid to pick up either her or Ellie for a date or to drop them off.

Stevie was brought up to marry a Catholic, bear children, and serve her family, just as her mother had for fifty long years with a husband who was mean and stern and who had beat her and the children. At sixteen, however, my mother got pregnant. I doubt anyone ever knew this except her and my grandmother. My grandmother took her to New Jersey for an abortion, afraid that if her father found out he would kill both her and Stevie. My grandmother believed that if any man my mother met after that found out about the abortion, he would "run away and never come back," and she grew nervous that her daughter would never marry. When my mother then got pregnant with me, my grandmother took her to a priest for advice. The priest suggested an abortion, but this time my mother refused.

My mother had met my father at a dance at the Mayfair Hotel in "the City," and within three weeks they were married. Eddy had not wanted to get an apartment for them, only hotel rooms, and he had her take out a loan for $300 to finance them. Upon learning that my mother was pregnant, he made it clear that he had no use for, nor interest in, a girl child. If I was a boy, he told my mother, she should let him know. If not, she needn't bother. By this time, she had learned that he was a bigamist and had the marriage annulled. Eddy was deported.

Unmarried, alone, and left with my father's debts, my mother moved back home and got a job as a waitress while my grandmother took care of me. Then she met a restaurant manager named Jeff at church, and married him after a couple of months of dating. My grandmother was relieved, even jubilant, that Jeff had married my mother. I was six months old at the time.

Life with Jeff as a part of our family is when my memories began, although to this day, most of them are vague and darkly elusive, like shadows in fog. My mother told me later that Jeff didn't like when I cried, and when I did he put a pillow over my face to muffle the sound. I remember his jet-black hair, his violent temper, and his hatred of me. The most vivid memory—like it was yesterday—is of me with my brown, nappy hair locked out on the back porch in snow that was taller than I was. The bottom half of the door was wood and the top was glass. Hard as I tried, I just couldn't make myself tall enough to see inside. I could hear my mother crying while being hit and knocked down to the cold, wooden floor. Hours later, the door finally opened and her broken body struggled to close her arms about me, get me in, and get me warm. I wasn't yet three years old when this happened.

Jeff moved us to North Carolina when I was still a toddler. By the age of four, I knew well the meaning of absolute fear and terror, as well as the ecstasy I felt during those short-lived weeks when Jeff was away on business. Supposedly he was a traveling Bible salesman. We grew to cherish his absence.

In 1958, my mother found out that Jeff, too, was a bigamist, married to a woman in Virginia. By then, she had given birth to my two brothers, Nate and Jonathan.

CHAPTER 11
San Antonio and Harvey

My mother left Jeff and North Carolina behind. She drove in her Ford Fairlane 500 with three babies, our clothes, and ten dollars to her name, bound for San Antonio, where Aunt Ellie lived. I was five, Nate was three-and-a-half, and Jonathan was nine months old. Aunt Ellie had had about as much luck with men as my mother. She too was a single and divorced mother. She had a two-year-old girl named Angie and later another daughter, Melanie, and son, Freddie.

San Antonio was a home. Finally, a place where we felt safe, loved, noticed, secure, and profoundly relieved. My mother started waitressing again, and I began to clean, cook, feed, bathe, and take care of my brothers and cousins. It felt like playing house, but it was a happy house. I so desperately hoped my mother would never marry again.

Life was perfect from my point of view, but below the happy surface and hidden from me were the struggles my mother faced being single, young, and naïve. She wasn't making enough money to feed us and briefly resorted to prostitution. She was arrested and sent to jail for four hours because someone, as she recalled, "ratted" on her. The same woman who had turned her in helped her get a lawyer, and my mother was able to get off with a $25 fine. Of course, the lawyer's help was on condition that she sleep with him, despite her telling him she had been charging for sex to feed her children.

When my mother wrote this and we talked about it later, I learned she had never told anyone about having to prostitute herself. It was as if she had been waiting all her life, she said, for someone to tell of her experiences, her dreams, her pain, and her secrets. This revelation made something ugly into one of many precious, healing experiences of sharing, for both of us.

She and Aunt Ellie both worked and between them had three kids who were not in school yet. They hired a black maid named Nellie, who lived with us for five or six years. It was the late 1950s, and in the South, it was common for white families to have black maids. Bigotry and racism were rampant. The lines in Nellie's face etched years of hardship and suffering, but if she held any bitterness, it never came across in her actions or words. She was up every day at 4:00 a.m., cooking breakfast feasts for us and reading the Bible. When we acted out, she took her shoe off and chased us around the house play-hollering, "Shoe, get 'em!" Her love for us was obvious, as was ours for her.

Sometime during the early 1960s, Mom met Harvey, a retired county sheriff and minister in the Church of Christ. He was a southern, mild-mannered Texan. Until he came into my life, I don't remember ever going to church, even though I had been christened in the Catholic faith as an infant and my mother said we were Catholic.

Harvey was in his fifties—over twenty years older than my mother—and nearly bald, with a big, drooping stomach and skinny legs. He was kind and compassionate. Soon I began to sense that he wasn't going to beat anyone. I was right. My mother described him as a tender, caring man, and a great lover who took her away on romantic weekends.

As a preacher's eldest daughter (he legally adopted my brothers and me), I assumed increasing responsibilities after Nellie left to work for another family. I even helped teach Bible study class to kids younger than I. Harvey was the first male person in our lives to teach my brothers and me about morality, humility, gratitude, and generosity. These lessons I would later abandon, but they somehow remained deeply ingrained in me underneath thick layers of emotional and psychological damage.

My mother got a job at Southern Pacific Railroad and worked nights as a billing clerk, while Harvey was on paid disability and received a stipend for his work in the church. My mother then received money from her father's estate when he died. We were living better than we ever had.

We moved to Tucson, Arizona, where Harvey had been offered a part-time job as a preacher, and for the first time, my mother was able to buy a house. We spent Sunday mornings and nights, as well as Wednesday nights, in church, and the boys and I went to church camps during the summer months.

Unfortunately, Harvey had serious heart problems and had undergone three open-heart surgeries. Refusing to stick to a salt-free diet, he would raid the refrigerator in the wee hours of the morning while everyone slept. I learned later that he drank heavily, too. As his health worsened, at the tender young age of eight or nine, I became a nursemaid to him in addition to caregiver to my brothers. He was bedridden almost the entire last year of his life. While my mother worked nights, I worked days, nights, and weekends at being all grown up and responsible. I was a model child and honor student, passionate about reading and learning. I was safe. We all were, and it was so different from what we had known before Harvey came into our lives.

Childhood is a paradox to me. I often think of a scene in the Barbra Streisand movie *Nuts* where she is on the stand in a courtroom being hammered about whether she had a good childhood. She quietly whispers in response, "I don't believe in childhood." I'm not sure I do either. I don't remember much of it. I think it was stolen before I could talk or walk.

CHAPTER 12
Hell Is for Children:
Rape, 1964

By age eleven, and with a few years void of terror and violence at home, I was content in our little family routine. I actually felt a sense of safety and happiness. I had gotten good at mastering everything required and expected of me. I was smart, competent, and a "good girl" who cared deeply about my family and friends.

One September day, walking home from school to my eastside home in the desert, I saw a brigade of cars parked around the house. I immediately sensed tragedy and knew something was very wrong. Harvey had died. That was the first time I experienced the death and loss of someone significant to me. Grief-stricken, I couldn't believe God had taken him from us, and I denounced God that day. I kept Harvey's last name until I met my own father much later, as well as so much of what he had given us and me.

Even though we were devastated by Harvey's death, things at home were stable. My mother received Social Security benefits for all of us. She kept her job and stayed single for a brief time. We were all sad, but his life and death had brought our family even closer, however short-lived it was.

The steadiness of our family's life was shattered again, as soon as my mother met Manny. I prayed to the God I had denounced when Harvey died that Manny wouldn't move in, and if he did, that he would be nice. He did move in, only two months after she had met him. My mother continued to work nights, and Manny didn't work at all.

At first, he was great fun. He drank beer and became silly, playful, and generous. The boys and I were so excited when we found out she was going to marry him. He was a great dancer and I remember watching him and my mother dreamily dancing to "Strangers in the Night." They were a stunning couple.

But before long, Manny's true colors shone through. He spent most nights lying in a green recliner in front of the TV, inebriated, and barking orders at me to bring him food or drink. The silly, playful man had disappeared. One night while my mother was at work, he came to my bed drunk. I remember how hard it was not to cry out, to scream, but I didn't want my brothers to hear. The graphic details of that night, I don't remember, but I know I experienced panic, guilt, and confusion after Manny raped me. Terror stood out as my biggest reaction.

After he left my room and passed out, I packed a thin white pillow-case with a change of clothes, some bread and bologna, and, of course, my most prized and favorite possession, the 45 rpm of "Monday, Monday" by the Mamas and Papas. Strange, the things I thought I would need to survive. Where to run? I had no idea, but just knew I had to. How could something so wrong and so vile have happened to me, a preacher's daughter?

Manny's two daughters from a previous marriage were Mary Helen, who was eighteen years old, and Carmen, nineteen. I had met them both and loved hanging out with them. They were older, cool, and hip. I went to a phone booth in the dark of night and called Mary Helen. I told her I had just run away and why. She told me to stay put, came and got me, and accompanied me to the police station.

The police told Mary Helen to take me to juvenile hall, a place called Old Mother Higgins. I spent the night there, alone in a cold, steel, barren isolation cell. The next morning in an interrogation room with Manny, my mother, a social worker, and the police officer who had taken my statement the night before, I recounted the vague details I could remember of the rape. Manny glared at me and when I finished, he denied everything. My mother said nothing. I was sent home, sentenced to a continuation of Manny's physical and verbal abuse, fueled now with his angry vengeance toward me. He never raped me again, but he beat me from then on, for the next seven years, until I went to juvenile prison just before I turned eighteen.

It was that day, that morning after the rape, when I felt my heart begin to harden. During the ride home in the car with them from Old Mother Higgins, I knew deep down that I had been altered forever. Any childhood innocence I clung to before that day was gone. My mother's silence, the dead quiet in the car, sealed the loss like dirt over a coffin. It was then I began to stifle my pain, my emotions, and my terrible fear of the man my mother had married.

I felt so confused about my mother. No matter how despicable the men she married were, I knew she loved us. I knew it deep down. She told me years later that when Manny started drinking and hitting us, she tried to leave several times, but then lost her job when she got pregnant with my precious baby sister, Jeanette (there was no such thing as the Family Medical Leave Act then). Meanwhile, Manny quit one job after another, getting worse and sicker each year. My mother said she couldn't stand him after a while, but could not afford to move (there were also no domestic violence laws in the 1960s).

I understood her passiveness, her failure to take aggressive action against the violator of her children. She didn't know anything else. For my part, I didn't fault her consciously, but I see now that for the next twenty years of my life, I acted out my anger over not being protected by self-destructing. In so doing, I punished myself and everyone who loved me, including my mother.

I knew her fear of Manny was as great as mine. When she stepped in to stop him, he beat her too. I wanted to protect her, and I wanted to protect my brothers, but I was too small. I listened to him call her names like "pig," "bitch," and "stupid." I hated this more than his beating me. Even at my young age, I saw and understood why beaten and broken women stay with their abusers. They become emotionally paralyzed from the constant rejection, terror, and humiliation. More often than not, these women come from families with intergenerational histories of abuse. In the case of my own mother, she also suffered from severe financial limitations, and during that time, there were no such things as shelters for battered women and children.

Manny was one of fourteen siblings. Although his mother—my step-grandmother—spoke only Spanish, I could sense that she knew what he was doing to me, at least the beatings. Although I never had a real conversation with her about it, I knew she knew, and for some reason I found that a bit comforting. We had many aunts, uncles, and cousins on his side of the family, and through those years, we adopted many Mexican customs. We cooked tamales every Christmas Eve, ate menudo on New Year's Day, and went to plenty of Quinceañeras, huge family gatherings to celebrate a Hispanic girl's turning fifteen years old, where all the men got insanely drunk and into fights while we kids snuck beer, wine, and liquor. Within that large family, I later realized, more than a few long-suffering, emotionally paralyzed wives knew their children were being hurt, but could not or would not do anything to stop it.

When Mom finally divorced Manny, he told her she would never make it. But she did make it, and stood by him through his last years in spite of how he had treated her. I never knew her to carry malice or hatred in her heart, for anyone. When Manny died, he was bedridden, in pain and alone except for a few scarce relatives, Mom, and his daughter. He had severe diabetes and had developed gangrene in his legs to the point where one was amputated. Later, my mother said she thought the Lord had disciplined him for his sins, but she knew she had also made mistakes. She said that she hoped we, her children, would always think of her as she did her own mother, with no blame. Her pure and undying love for us somehow made up for what he did. She said she felt thankful, privileged, and humbled to have us as her children. It would take a long time for me to evolve and find that same humility she had instilled in me by the way she had carried and conducted herself throughout her life. I now know what a privilege it was to have her as my mother.

Those were the days of Twiggy, Bianca Jagger, and Marianne Faithful. In terms of fashion and what was in, I wasn't even close. My manner of dress was peculiar. Most girls my age wore Villager skirts and Capezio shoes with cutesy cardigan sweaters. I had none of these kinds of clothes, and didn't have much of a sense of style anyway. I have since learned that lack of fashion or style sense is an Aquarian trait, if astrology is to be believed.

By age thirteen, I had crooked teeth, still-nappy hair, and a big nose. I was nerdy and awkward in my prepubescent skin, and on top of all this, I had thick, black hair on my legs that Manny forbade me to shave. If I did, I was beaten. I wore knee socks to cover them, even when it was 110 degrees outside, which was months at a time during most years in Arizona. I suffered beatings at home and ridicule at school.

This is it, my life, I concluded. I dreaded it most of the time.

CHAPTER 13
Heroin: It's My Wife, It's My Life

Tucson during the 1960s was a town abundant with drugs, which were brought over from Nogales, a small border town in Mexico only sixty miles away. One crowd at school was using a lot of them, and the girls in that group weren't wearing Villager skirts and Capezios, but rather fringed leather vests, T-shirts, Levi's, and boots or sandals. This style, typical of the era, was a much better fit for me. However, Manny forbade me to wear jeans, so I had to sneak out of the house every morning in a dress and take my cool clothes in my school bag to change into in the school bathroom. When he caught me—more than once—he pounded on me. One particular day, he dragged me by my hair from the living room to my bedroom, slamming the door behind him and ordering me to change clothes.

By the seventh grade, I had tried pot. And in an instant, I had found an out from the nose, the hair, the crooked teeth, the hairy legs and knee socks, the ugly realities of my life. Like magic, when I took drugs, it didn't matter how homely or weird I was. I was instantly accepted, and being hit at home no longer affected my emotions, only my body. Being high even eased the pain of those bruises and welts a little.

My baby sister, Jeanette, was born two days before my fourteenth birthday, and I still think of her as my fourteenth birthday present. With my mother working nights, I was Jeanette's surrogate mother. I adored her and raised her for the most part until she was five, but within an environment where toddlers were charged with getting and opening cans of beer and passing joints for people who were too stoned to move. They would sip the alcohol, too, as all of us were oblivious to its harmful effects on these innocent babies.

Denise Sassoon

Drugs were not only pleasurable but also lucrative. I started buying ounces of pot and rolling the ounces into joints, forty or fifty a bag, and selling them for twenty-five or fifty cents at school and in my neighborhood. It wasn't long before I got into heavier drugs: LSD, Black Beauties, and downers like Seconal and Nembutal ("reds" and "yellows").

The niche I had carved for myself was working. I was notorious at school as a "head" or "stoner," I was respected and admired among my newfound crowd, and Jeanette was the absolute light of my life. Aside from Manny, all seemed well. My mother sometimes talked him into taking her out dancing, while behind his back she helped me organize parties for all my friends. She and I hid the liquor in the washing machine until they left to go dancing. According to our plan, she would call a half-hour before they were coming home, giving me time enough to end the party and clear everyone out. And parties they were. We had everything from Heineken beer and acid-laced wine to pot and heroin. It was the height of the 1960s, an awesome, innocent, and wild time.

On a hill in Himmel Park on weekends, any drug, any time, was free. It was powerful, this subculture of peace, love, and dope. Pink Floyd's *Dark Side of the Moon* was the album of the times for doing acid. The music of the Rolling Stones, Jimi Hendrix, and Janis Joplin was perfect for drunken bashes. Al Green was a "must" for sex.

As the violence increased at home, I became Manny's main target. I figured that he didn't beat my brothers as often or as severely because he knew one day they would grow big enough to get him back. The higher I got, though, the less painful were Manny's black boots and angry fists, flailed at me at home or in restaurants and other public places. He didn't care where we were when he hit me. As I look back, I cringe at the apathy of those strangers who witnessed this and looked the other way. No one ever said anything or tried to stop it. The marks of his attacks on me progressed from cuts, welts, and bruises to broken bones. I was in and out of school. I had pretty much abandoned studying, got kicked out of three high schools, and mostly just hung out in parking lots and parks to deal drugs. If I did go to class, it was to do business. And business was booming.

In my freshman year of high school, undercover narcotics agents raided sewing class to arrest me. I had been seen passing a joint to someone. I was charged with sales and carted off to Old Mother Higgins, which by then was my second home anyway. I ran away from home as often as I could, but always got sent back there and charged with being "incorrigible" each time, even though I always told the authorities about the beatings. Domestic violence was not a crime then, and in fact, the police who witnessed the effects and aftermath of it could do nothing. Ironic that if the men who beat their wives or children did the same to a stranger, only then was it treated as a crime.

I was getting busted at least twice a year and all the while getting and staying as high as I could. I was snorting, injecting, buying, selling, and keestering drugs. During about a two-year period starting when I was sixteen, I ate LSD every day. It took me to wondrous places. I wish I could have saved some of those trips to somehow recall again at will. Of the many things I regret having done, taking LSD is not among them. One LSD experience turned a road trip to Sierra Vista—in an orange 1965 Volkswagen bug, driving through the spring desert with its distant, purple mountains against an endless azure sky—into a moving, flowing cartoon. It was amazing and brilliant, and I've never forgotten the colors and textures of all those LSD trips. LSD stretched the boundaries of my mind in a way that nothing else could, and to expand the mind out that far was to see things many never would.

By age sixteen, I was a dedicated, full-fledged, game-for-anything, dope fiend. During one of my Mom-and-Manny-out-dancing house parties, two college-aged, hippie guys standing in the bathroom asked me if I wanted to join them. They were shooting heroin. They didn't have to ask twice. One of them tied me off with a bandana and the other shot me up. It fit and felt perfect, more perfect than anything I'd ever felt, even better than sex with Steve, the high school sweetheart I had met freshman year and was with all throughout high school. Both virgins (with the exception of Manny's attack in my case), Steve and I taught each other how to make love, drink, and do more drugs. His gentle innocence and sweet lovemaking staved off some of the damage my stepfather had done when he desecrated my young body.

Within a few months, I fell into the abyss of heroin. Steve and most friends my age weren't doing heroin. They were more into pot, acid, and alcohol, not so much the hard drugs yet, and I kept my heroin use hidden for nearly two years. But after heroin, there was no other drug for me, other than maybe a good joint right after fixing, which gave it a kick, or shooting some crystal or coke followed by heroin, which makes crashing from either of those easy and soothing.

One of the things I regret most during this time was my loose attitude toward drugs. Like other stoners, I regarded them as a "gift." This translated into my letting my baby sister, only two or three years old at the time, take sips of beer and pass joints around to everyone. I also regret introducing my brother Jonathan to drugs. Nate was using, too, but liked to drink more than anything. Jonathan was more like me, game for anything. Later this would bring grave consequences to us both. At this point, all of us except Jeanette were being beaten. Manny had overcome his fear of the boys, and it seemed he was spiraling out of control over his violent impulses.

After I had been arrested for incorrigibility countless times, my parents and probation officer sent me to live with Manny's relatives in Fontana, California. The rationale was that I needed to be out of Tucson. That didn't work. There, I was seen as the "black sheep" and accused of being a negative influence on my cousins, even though most of them were already using something, too. After a few short months, I was sent back to Tucson.

One year, after Manny had lost yet another job, we were nearly starving and lost our home. He devastated my mother financially. Even though she was working, as she always had, we were living in poverty, and I had just been busted again. On the advice of my probation officer, Mom and Manny decided to move the whole family to Key West, Florida, where my Aunt Ellie lived. My mother hadn't seen her in years and missed her a lot. The family used my issues as an excuse, telling me we were moving because of my drug use. But the truth was that we were soon to be homeless because of Manny if we didn't do something drastic.

For the first month or so, we stayed at Aunt Ellie's. Then we moved into a single-wide trailer in what felt like swampland in the middle of summer. I was terrified of the variety and size of the bugs, and the humidity was beyond oppressive. Mom got a job, but predictably, Manny did not. He heard about jobs on the shrimp docks, where it didn't matter what age you were. Supposedly, they paid $1.50 per full bucket of shrimp heads. He sent us kids to check it out and report back. When we came home and told him it was true, he put all three of us to work for the rest of the summer heading shrimp. Jonathan and Nate were both less than ten years old. The sharp edges of the shells combined with the acid in the shrimp mangled our young hands. My brothers stood crying beside the conveyer belt, but kept popping the heads off those shrimp. I watched them, once again feeling helpless. Witnessing that filled me with an even uglier hatred for Manny. I despised him for doing that to the boys!

In the end, Florida didn't work out. Once again we were evicted, and we returned to Tucson. My mother got her old job back at the railroad and somehow we got by, no thanks to Manny.

Two weeks before I turned eighteen, Steve threw me a birthday party. He still had no clue that I was doing heroin daily, hourly on some days. My habit necessitated that I wear long sleeves to cover my tracks, odd that he never noticed that in a town where 105 degrees is so common. But heroin addicts are resourceful when it comes to the secret ritual of injecting their drug. They keep their rig, spoon, tie, cotton, and lighter in a make-up bag, sock, or purse, so they can tie off and "fix" (shoot the heroin intravenously) anywhere—in cars, behind buildings, in the bathrooms of restaurants or gas stations—and do so in less than five minutes. No one around them is the wiser for it.

I had waited so long to be eighteen because it meant I could leave home and be free of Manny, without being charged as an incorrigible runaway and sent to Old Mother Higgins. But my heroin habit drained me of any money I might have used to move, so I was stuck. I didn't relish the idea of having to crash here and there, and I felt overwhelmed and desperate without money or a plan. But the sweet, delicious, sacred, secret ritual of cooking up my fix, getting a register, then descending softly and slowly to euphoria overshadowed any desperation I had, at least while I was high.

Around that time, Jimi Hendrix, Janis Joplin, and Jim Morrison all died within two years of each other. For me, this touched off an obsession with death. I envied them in their quiet peace, seeing them as strong and courageous enough to end their misery. I wanted to go out like them, to simply drift into final oblivion.

In this state of mind, right before my birthday party, I fixed a big hit of heroin at home and ate a handful of Seconals, knowing it was a lethal combination. I didn't care. I remember being on a couch next to Steve and then the ride to the hospital in the back of his Dodge Dart as I lay across his lap. At the hospital, they rushed me into a bay after Steve told them I had overdosed. Apparently, he knew more than I thought he did. I remember feeling as though I was floating away from the room, and then abruptly waking up to the taste of charcoal in my mouth. Back then, it was the treatment used for an overdose. They saved me, damn them! Because I was a minor, my parents were notified and came to pick me up. Awakened by Manny, my mother, and the police, I was being arrested for possession of heroin and pot Manny had found in my room. He had turned me in.

***

I had been on probation since I was twelve, and my probation officer was tired of my empty promises, my failure to follow through on my good intentions, but most of all my wasted potential. She recommended to the court that I be sent to juvenile prison, a place in Phoenix called Good Shepherd. It was a state institution for girls run by Catholic nuns. It didn't bother me that I was sentenced to a year there. I figured it couldn't be much worse than juvenile hall or home.

Even though I had been using heroin for several months without a break, I did not experience withdrawal during my forced abstinence at Good Shepherd. With heroin, it takes a while for physical dependence to set in. I still wanted to get high, but drugs were few and far between at Good Shepherd.

While in juvenile prison, I met young girls who had been beaten up by life. I could see it in their cold, hard, vacant eyes. And like me, these girls were disillusioned about life, the world, everything, and did drugs as a way out. We learned a lot together at Good Shepherd. We learned not to cry and how to hate. We learned harsh lessons about cruelty and racism within the context of this prison world where they thrived. We learned how to fool the nuns and defy authority and that you had to play whatever hand you were dealt. We learned to make prison our home, which in most cases was better than where we had come from. Also, the light of education was available in the academic lessons the Catholic nuns taught us. Education was one of my saving graces throughout many years of upheaval and self-destruction.

While there, I took advantage of a nurses' aide training program that allowed me to go offsite my last few months for on-the-job training at a nursing home. I loved it. Even though I wasn't getting paid, it was my first real job other than the brief stints I had done in restaurants as a waitress or bus girl in my teens. So I decided to become a nurse. When I paroled, an ex-offender program paid for me to go to nursing school. I was energized, motivated, and fairly impressed with my newfound ability to earn honors grades, make the Dean's list, and pass the State Board licensing exam. I wasn't doing heroin, and as far as I was concerned, that meant I was clean. To me and almost every other heroin addict I met, other drugs didn't "count," only heroin.

Meanwhile, Steve and I tried rekindling our flame, only to discover it had died. We had both changed. Faithfully, he had waited for me that entire year, graduating high school and then working in his father's carpentry business. Steve was still that soft, gentle, laid-back hippie. I was also, but much less so because I had donned a protective shell and edge, a hardened heart, and an unrelenting appetite for drugs. My perfect high school romance ended.

Eventually, I got my dream job in a nursing home as a licensed practical nurse. I worked the 3:00 to 11:00 evening shift there for about a year. The job came with excellent benefits, namely, access to as many Class A narcotics and shiny new syringes (or fits or rigs, as they were sometimes called) as I wanted. At the time, Quaaludes were all the rage and hadn't yet been classified as Class A narcotics, so they weren't inventoried. I was taking and giving those away by the handfuls. For my friends, I scored Seconal, Nembutal, and Digoxin, and for me, mostly Demerol, Morphine, and Dilaudid. The opiates were counted, and before they were administered, they had to be signed off with another nurse as a witness. Thus, the only option for stealing them was to switch them with other pills that looked the same before giving them to the patients. If the patient was receiving shots, then I replaced the drug with water and gave myself the shot. Shameless behavior, as I look back on it, but not unusual.

I never got caught taking drugs from work, but the dream job sort of faded away, or I did. Before long, I was off and running again. Up to this point, I hadn't yet suffered withdrawal or experienced the full effect of kicking heroin. Having heard of and seen others go through its living hell, I attempted to stay away from that drug. Thanks to the nursing job, other narcotics had been readily available to (somewhat) ease the separation from heroin. It helped that they were opiates, but still, like the longing for an old yet unforgotten lover, my desire to reunite with my favorite high had only been buried, not extinguished.

CHAPTER 14
Falling, I Keep Falling…

My permanent default mechanism, drugs, resumed their place as the main feature of my existence, my life force. I lived and worked for them. I knew it would be almost effortless for me to make a living selling drugs (and using them, but heroin only occasionally, of course). For a brief time, I took up again with LSD, use of which was still rampant within the drug culture.

My tripping partner much of that time was Marci, my best friend. An attractive brunette with sparkling hazel eyes and long hair almost to her waist, she was the embodiment of hippie beauty, especially with her wardrobe of Spanish-style gauze blouses trimmed with vibrant embroidery, lots of turquoise jewelry, and of course Levi's and sandals. Marci and I were into being peace-and-love children, that and doing acid, mescaline, pot, and pills. One night while on LSD, we decided to hitchhike to the East Coast to hang out on the beach in New Jersey. It was still relatively safe to hitchhike then and thus began an eight-month adventure meeting other hippies like us, mostly families and religious fanatics living in communes.

We also met many truck drivers, who out of everyone we encountered were the most bizarre. They could also be extremely dangerous. Somewhere in Oklahoma, we were picked up by a scraggly looking trucker with a pot belly. In the cab of his truck, he kept eying us from beneath his messy, gray eyebrows. He said he could take us further east, but first wanted to stop at a friend's place where we could all eat dinner. We agreed reluctantly, mainly because we were starving. When we got to his friend's small apartment, however, we discovered that instead of dinner there were just a bunch of peculiar-acting people. I wasn't sure what they were on, but no one was talking much. There were more men than women, and most of them looked like they might be in their fifties. They seemed to be aimlessly wandering about the place, looking unsure why they were there or what they were doing. Marci and I immediately felt uncomfortable as they regarded us with creepy, vacant stares. Our instincts on alert, we knew to get out of there quickly and did.

Another time, in the backwoods of Arkansas, we hitched a ride with a truck driver who kept traveling further away from the main highway, all the while telling us he was taking a shortcut. After forty minutes of no civilization, lights, or traffic, we were unnerved and asked him to stop the truck so we could get out. He didn't, and just kept driving. When he refused to stop after two more requests, we started screaming at him hysterically, and thankfully, he finally let us out. We shot out of the cab—at 3:00 a.m. in pouring rain—and sprinted through the dark woods to escape from him. By our luck or his laziness, he kept driving. The remainder of the trip was uneventful; we got rides with like-minded hippies, smoking pot, dropping acid, and drinking wine merrily along the way.

Once we reached New Jersey, we met a woman named Jane. She was an older, frumpy-looking lady, but she had a place and offered to let us stay with her. Back then, it was never a problem finding a place to crash. We wound up staying with Jane all summer in Cape May, living on the second floor of a beautiful, old Victorian house on a block lined on both sides with luscious white oak, tulip, and dogwood trees. Cape May was, like many other small US towns, going through the 1960s revolution and was a great party town.

After our cross-country hitchhiking trip, we wound up back in Tucson, where we amused ourselves by playing in the snow on Mount Lemon barefoot and topless, and staying awake for days on end painting flowers on our walls. Once in a while, we dated guys, but we were just as content without them, getting high and listening to Joan Baez, Barbra Streisand, Carly Simon, and Joni Mitchell in our happy, little hippie home. We even pierced Marci's nose one night while we were both on mushrooms. Frankly, I was in love with her, but my religious underpinnings did not permit such deviant thoughts, so the relationship remained platonic.

Living with Marci came to an end one summer when we went to Delaware, Ohio, a tiny college town where she had an ex-boyfriend from school named Darrell. He let us crash at his house for a few weeks. Darrell was over six feet tall, gangly, and resembled pictures of Jesus with long shiny, brownish/blond hair and a full moustache and beard. Over this time, Marci and Darrell fell back in love and got engaged. Once we were back in Tucson, Marci gathered her things and moved to Ohio. Marci and Darrell proceeded to have three beautiful, blond daughters, all born within about a year of each other. Years later, I went to visit them. By that time, they had been "born again" and were devout disciples of one of the many religious cults so common throughout the country. Darrell seemed like a good and decent man who treated Marci well, but I never really understood how Marci had gone from being such a free spirit to the Christian version of a Stepford wife. Certainly her eyes had lost the light and mischief I had known, and I couldn't help but think of the movie *Frances*, starring Jessica Lange, which tells the story of Frances Farmer, a woman actually lobotomized because of her feisty personality. Nevertheless, if Marci was happy, I was happy for her.

Jonathan came to live with me after Marci left, driven away from Mom's house by Manny. He was almost fifteen years old, and I swore I could take care of him and give him a better life than he had at home. He was popular in school, athletic, and good-looking. He was quite the lady's man too; girls swooned over him. Sadly, though, my own drug use was like a contagious disease, and I ended up turning him on to mainlining heroin. In the beginning, we were using mainly on weekends.

At school, Jonathan met a beautiful Hispanic girl named Liz, who came from a family of major-league drug traffickers. Liz's mother was the kingpin, and she took a liking to Jonathan and me. One day he came home from school, delighted with something Liz's brother, Miguel, had given him to sell. From his pocket he pulled the first full ounce of pure uncut heroin I had ever seen, an exquisite, amber-colored gem.

Right away we prepared for the shooting-up ritual. Jonathan had already fixed and was across the room getting a cigarette. I was just ready to fix myself when I heard him fall and ran over to find him, lying face-up on the floor, lips gone blue. Shock and panic seized me as I tried unsuccessfully to bring him back. Oh, my God, my baby brother! Overdosed! I screamed for help. Some neighbors that we partied with came over and tried to help me revive him, to no avail. We called 911. The paramedics came and took him by ambulance to the hospital.

They revived my brother, but no longer could I deny the seriousness of the consequences of my drug use. There are certain defining moments in every life, and this was one of mine, knowing that Jonathan had nearly died at my hands.

Tragically, however, it was too late. We had fallen into addiction and there was no turning back.

Miguel and I were the same age, about eighteen, when Jonathan and I started working for him and "the family." The work was simple, selling heroin and cocaine. We were quick studies and soon became wildly successful. The dope we were getting was coming from Culiacan, eighty percent pure, and the best anyone could get around Tucson. Business was booming. We could cut one ounce into three or four because of the quality, which translated to a 300 or 400 percent profit margin (plus unlimited amounts of coke and heroin to do ourselves). And overnight, it seemed, Jonathan and I were rich. Not even twenty years old, we had enough money to pay cash for cars and move into a high-end home. Our house was open all hours of the night for fortune-seeking, hungry, and sick customers.

Shooting coke was a new experience for us. The rush . . . well, there is nothing like it, no words to describe it. But that high took us to a deeper level of desperation as we constantly sought to top the last hit. With either coke or heroin, a good hit meant you immediately threw up, but it was worth it for what came after. If Liz's mother had known we were using, she would have fired us. The ground rule of being in her employ was that selling was okay, but using was not.

Miguel knew we were shooting dope, but instead of ratting on us, he was curious and asked us to let him try it. Before long, he also started mainlining both heroin and cocaine, and this completely altered him. Within a few months, he started having paranoid psychotic episodes when he shot cocaine, during which he would accuse us of ripping off his family. From our aspect, there was no reason to rip them off. We were rolling in money and dope. Eventually, he realized we weren't stealing from them, but only after a harrowing encounter with him while on the way to the airport on a day we were flying to Boston with two ounces of heroin. Especially agitated that day, Miguel pulled a gun on us in the car. We showed him the several thousand dollars we had, and reminded him we had just paid for the dope we were taking to Boston. He relented and then started laughing hysterically. We weren't as amused.

About eight months later, Liz's mother called us to her house early one morning. She said Miguel had gone into her bedroom, sat at the foot of her bed, and shot himself in the head. She was devastated with shock and grief, but nothing stopped the business over which she was the top boss. Shortly after he died, she summoned us to her house to let us know she was sending us to Nogales in Sonora, Mexico. There, we were to meet her eldest son, Pasqual, who would give us further instructions. Entering Mexico was easy, and Pasqual took us to a house where I saw more drugs than I had ever seen. There must have been three or four kilos of heroin and cocaine stored in that place! Jonathan and I sensed that it would be better for us to act cool, as if it was no big thing, but our hearts were racing at the sight of that much dope. Pasqual asked whether we knew about keestering. We assured him we did, and this seemed to ease the tension. He winked at us as if to say we had given him a good answer. In all, we keestered a quarter pound between us that night, and within three weeks, we became skilled at the game. Smuggling drugs into the US and flying them to the East Coast was easy for us. With the exception of a few nights, we ran the border every night for nearly a year.

Jonathan and I were two youngsters, preacher's kids, straight-up gangsters, addicts, and now drug smugglers. Our habits, business, and bankrolls were moving fast, so fast.

One night, after we'd been running drugs for a few months, we went to Nogales to pay Pasqual $4,000 and pick up another batch. His wife met us at the door, a tragic and stricken look on her face, and waved us away without taking the money. We went to the house where he kept the dope and learned he had been beaten, shot, and left to die in a ditch. The story was that he owed some people further south a lot of money, got in over his head, and wound up paying with his life. He left his wife and eight children behind.

By then, we had gotten to know a few other people and went to see another connection we had met. We bought an ounce of heroin and a half-ounce of coke, but were advised that the Federales were in town and that we should stay on the Mexico side that night and wait until morning to cross the border. In our room at the El Cid, the best hotel in Nogales, Jonathan and I proceeded to shoot heroin and cocaine for the next sixteen hours, literally. The only break we took was to board a bus for the hour-long ride back to Tucson, but even on the old Greyhound Bus, we managed to fix in its skanky bathroom. Back home, still binging, shooting coke every five minutes, I looked across the kitchen table to see Jonathan, sticking the needle repeatedly into his already abscessed, bleeding arms. The inside of the syringe was the cloudy pink color of coagulated blood mixed with coke. Usually, I was the one who went through this because of my tiny veins, not him. Men have bigger veins and shooting dope is easier for them in general.

As I looked at Jonathan across that table, I experienced another brief, yet mercilessly raw and uncensored, moment of clarity and guilt. It was the same feeling of panic and hysteria I'd had when he overdosed. What had I done? This life I had created was no longer just about me. Now it was Jonathan, too—by day, a high school kid competing in statewide gymnastics tournaments, but by night, a drug-smuggling junkie following me down a path of destruction and despair. I've always marveled at how well junkies can pull off such parallel lives, and for so many years before they can no longer hide it.

One night a week later, Jonathan and I were home, along with a few customers and neighbors, when we were paid an unwelcome visit by three big-muscled men in ski masks. They kicked in our door and, pointing guns at us, ordered everyone down on the floor. After binding our mouths, ankles, and wrists with masking tape, they grabbed Jonathan by the hair, lifted him up, and demanded he show them where the money and drugs were. He resisted, but only briefly, as it was pretty clear they were dead serious about getting what they came for. They took about $3,000 and over an ounce of heroin. They didn't get any cocaine, only because there was never any left-over coke (we would always shoot that until it was gone). Before they left, they put us in the bedroom, closed the door, and ordered us not to come out until they were gone. Finally they departed, but not before ransacking the house, breaking televisions, stereos, windows, everything.

After that night, I couldn't rid myself of them, or rather, the fear of them. I was terrified to be at home alone. If Jonathan went out, I sat in Dunkin Donuts for hours if I had to until he got home. Our habits at this point were up to $400 or $500 a day. Miguel and Pasqual were dead. Even though we knew other connections, our booming business had come to an abrupt and untimely halt. We bought a gun and decided it would be best to move. Someone who worked with us or bought from us had set us up.

But we didn't move or reach our gun fast enough before the marauders came a second time. Again, Jonathan, a couple of customers, and I were at the house when they came, binding all of us with masking tape, lying us face down on the living room carpet—orange shag, of course—and telling us not to move. This time we only had about $500 and a quarter ounce of heroin, which infuriated the intruders. They refused to be convinced that was all we had, and I torturously watched as they beat Jonathan with the butt of a 37 Police Special. Meanwhile, a voice just over me behind a knife threatened to chop me up if I didn't give them the rest. It was too much. I lost control and began screaming and crying. I can't remember how long it was before I started to beg them to just go ahead and kill us. They finally left us broken down in pieces, in the dark, thick aftermath of a nightmare.

Somehow we scraped up enough money to move to the far north side of town. We stopped going to Mexico and were wiped out financially and emotionally. Physically, we finally learned the meaning of withdrawal. We woke up sick each day and spent every brutal waking moment trying to get well.

CHAPTER 15
The Mean Rape:
As If Any Aren't

1975. Saturday evening, the night before Easter. I was alone in the new apartment because Jonathan had gone to my mom's house for dinner. My usual precaution of leaving the house if Jonathan was gone was preempted by a hit so good that I couldn't even keep my eyes open, much less move. Earlier that day, we had scored two guns from a sick junkie so desperate to get well he had given them to us in exchange for a small amount of dope we still had at that point. Getting those guns had been an excellent deal for us, and we immediately used them in trade for $180 in food stamps, turquoise jewelry, and two $20 bags of heroin. After Jonathan and I shot the dope, I couldn't move from the couch. The front door was open, the screen unlocked, and the television blaring. What happened next was my greatest fear come to pass. In one slow blink of my eyes, the ski-masked men were inside my apartment.

By now I knew to expect the masking tape drill. Their deep voices and faces, even masked, were familiar. I could tell that one of them, slurring his words when he talked, was obviously drunk. He ranted and raved about another job they had done earlier in the day while the other two tried to quiet him down. When they pointed their guns at me and demanded drugs and money, I led them to the bedroom where I had the food stamps and jewelry. Like the time before, they didn't believe this was all I had and wanted more. But there was no more. So broken and wearied by what had become my life, I told them to do what they had to do. They grabbed my hair much the same way Manny used to do before he beat me, and dragged me to the living room. Flashing their guns and knives, they ripped a light blue phone from the wall and used the cord to tie my ankles and wrists.

The drunken one, becoming increasingly loud and belligerent, said, "Hey, I just did some coke, and I'm horny. What do you say we fuck her?"

"No man, that's not why we're here," answered another one.

"Fuck you, I'm going for it," said the drunk.

Fearing the neighbors would hear, the other two tried to settle him down and talk him out of it. But he persisted. "We gonna take something. She don't have no dope or money."

The other two agreed, seemingly if for no other reason than to shut him up. The drunken one went first, climbing onto me, one hand wielding his gun and the other covering my mouth to muffle my crying. One of the others closed the door, locked it, and went to the window to stand guard. While he penetrated my thin, limp body, the third one watched from the couch. Through the mask, my attacker's breath and mouth suffocated me. I closed my eyes and tried to stay calm outside, not let them see my fear. But inside, I felt my life, my world, my body being torn from me, taken to a place I'd been before by Manny, even though the memories were vague. It felt familiar, only this was so much worse.

I tried to block out the physical reality of it, but couldn't. The pain was beyond any realm of agony I had ever known. The drunken one finished, slithered off me, and motioned to the guy on the couch that it was his turn. He was fat and bigger than the first, and it hurt even more. I yearned to die, or if not die, at least to shut down. By the time the third one came, I was able to do what I had done with Manny for so long and just block it out. When the last one finished, I vaguely heard a casual laugh and a conversation about how ugly I was, that I was a pathetic junkie whore. Finally, they went away, leaving behind wreckage that never went away.

I was tied up, bleeding, bruised, and weak. Despite this, I had to get up, had to take a bath, and had to pull all the pieces of me back together before Jonathan came home. It didn't matter to me if he knew they had ripped us off again, but I couldn't reveal to him I had been raped by all three of them. I thought he was too innocent to hear this, although he really wasn't anymore. I couldn't imagine telling anyone, ever, and I didn't for over ten years. Like every rape victim I've ever met, I found a way to blame myself, caught in a tangle of guilt and shame. I was broken, damaged goods.

I have never understood what I did or did not do to deserve being raped. During the ten years of my silence about it, I told myself I had it coming for the lifestyle I had chosen, that it was all part of the game. Sometimes I convinced myself that it was punishment for what I had done to my baby brother. Before and even after finally talking about it, I would sometimes descend into a blackness of spirit and emotions. For a while, I was completely shattered. You don't ever recover from rape. It changes you in ways you cannot find language for. It still haunts me when I sleep. At those times, I wake up, silently screaming at the ski-masked men that creep into my dreams. To this day, I cannot be in a house alone, and I panic at night if the windows are not covered. These are the demons that may never retreat.

Many years later, I learned that there are men who don't hurt women and will even protect the women and children they love. I was fortunate enough to meet some of those men. Most importantly, though, I learned that after breaking my silence about the rape, a small degree of the fear subsided. Talking about the unspeakable gave others, both men and women, permission to speak of it too, and for that, I was grateful.

CHAPTER 16
The Arrest

The three weeks after I was attacked were a blur. Losing what little grip I had, I was slipping, slipping away. Inside, it felt as though all the different parts of me were trying to make sense and become one again, but could not. My thoughts were a tangled mass of lunacy. I was utterly convinced the masked men would come back.

I remember during this time that Jonathan and I, out of desperation, did things we had never done before. We were taking some guns to Mexico one day and stopped to drop off our rent, which we always paid in cash. We walked into the small leasing office and handed the money to a small, elderly woman wearing blue-rimmed glasses, the only person there. She put our rent money in her desk drawer, affording us a glimpse of the piles of cash and checks in there. We left the office, but on the spur of the moment realized how easy it would be to go back in and rob her. We always had bandanas in the car for when we had to tie off to shoot dope, and we used these to cover our mouths, bandit style. Conveniently, we had the guns for smuggling, and we borrowed one now to point at the office woman while demanding the money. I'll never forget how her hands shook and her lips trembled as she fumbled to gather the money quickly, pleading with us not to hurt her. Even in my crazy state of mind, it was crystal clear to me that she was just an innocent victim of our dire dependencies and that a line had just been crossed.

We had another scam of going into grocery stores and snatching purses. One of these belonged to a frail, old woman hunched over a walker. She never saw us coming. Her purse contained $3 in food stamps and some change. Certainly we had sunk to new lows. Jonathan was barely seventeen, and I was twenty. We were both so young, and yet not. We had already seen, lived, and done things we would learn from and regret, things for which amends would be required.

One day, an old connection came by and said she had been out of town a couple of years and wanted to score. We sold her two $20 bags. Two hours later, four Department of Public Safety undercover agents surrounded the house, kicked in the door, and put us on the couch at gunpoint while they searched the premises. They found a bag of pot and a sizable bag of dope, about a quarter ounce. We were charged with possession for sales of heroin and possession of marijuana, cuffed, arrested, and taken to jail. We both got released the next morning on our own recognizance under the condition that we get help for our drug problems. Jonathan and I returned home with no money and no dope, doubled over in the throes of withdrawal.

We sold Jonathan's beloved hunting rifle and copped enough dope to get well. I felt utterly wretched, afraid all the time, and strung out (physically weak and sick if deprived of a drug, and not able to feel high even after using). A pretrial worker at the jail had mentioned a place called Casa de Vida, a live-in program for heroin addicts. I made a decision to give this a try.

I will never forget the day I told Jonathan I was going away to live in this program. His blue eyes looked into mine with innocence, vulnerability, and a sense of being abandoned. By then, my mother and the rest of our family were beside themselves with helpless worry. Everyone's hearts were breaking. And now I was forsaking and losing my best friend and comrade in the world when he needed me the most. Guilt, remorse, shame, sorrow . . . none of these words adequately describes my feelings about what I had done to someone I loved so much.

Away I went to Casa de Vida. It was an old-school Therapeutic Community and extremely hard-core. The approach to treatment back then, peculiar to this model and particularly in the case of heroin addicts, was to break them down and force the feelings out of them. The staff was expected to bring these emotions to the surface by embarrassing, humiliating, and provoking the clients. There was little nurturing, but I kicked cold turkey. I didn't have much choice, because during my first week, the whole house went on a camping trip to the remote White Mountains in northern Arizona. It was hell, but

I survived and began to see, at first, that the people really were clean. Most of the staff were ex-addicts.

Even after all the harrowing recent events in my life, including the legal consequences of selling and using, I still couldn't wrap my mind around quitting heroin completely. But I did start to entertain the notion that at this point, with court pending, it was in my best interest to at least slow down. Jonathan had kicked cold turkey, too. After that, a social worker and a good friend of his took him under their wings and set him up with a job on Mount Lemmon helping to create trails for hikers and tourists. The job also provided him a small trailer in which to live. In addition, he took care of some horses for the manager of the stables at a resort hotel. It was the best thing that could have happened for Jonathan. He never shot heroin again. He later married, had three beautiful children, and became one of the best men, husbands, and fathers I have ever met. He remains a gentle, nurturing, strong, and caring man whose laughter can fill a room.

We were both assigned a public defender for the impending court date. This was my first encounter with the adult criminal justice system. I was advised to plead guilty to a lesser charge. My guilty plea was to possession of an amount of less than $250 as opposed to possession of an amount over that figure in worth (the actual amount I had had). Possession of the greater amount changed the charge to sales, and under the new mandatory sentencing law, the judge had no choice except to give a prescribed sentence of five flat years in prison. But with the reduced possession charge and plea bargain I was supposedly guaranteed, the judge had discretion to give me probation. A week before sentencing, my attorney came to the program to see me. He informed me I now had to plead guilty to the original charge because the prosecution was threatening a new charge, manslaughter. According to the prosecuting attorney, the last person I had sold to overdosed and died. So the deal was off the table. The attorney said I would still get probation and that it was unlikely they would pull me out of the program. I believed him. Oh, silly me.

***

1975. September 25, 2:00 p.m. I was standing in front of the Honorable Judge Alice Truman, daring to hope. All the staff and fifteen residents from the program were there to support me. But I didn't see anyone in my family, especially my mother! The judge's words echoed solemnly throughout the courtroom, in a voice stern and final. "No less than five, no more than fifteen years in the Arizona State Women's Prison at Florence," she said. Surely I had heard wrong! I turned around and read shock on the faces of my supporters. This was real. I was immediately handcuffed and put in a holding tank in the basement of the courthouse. On the way down, when the elevator opened on the first floor, there was my mother and baby sister, Jeanette. I cried out to them that I got five years. My mother reached out to console me, but the two police escorts snatched us apart.

In the holding tank, I made a poor second attempt to take my life. I cut my wrists with the only thing I had, a bobby pin. They took me to the county hospital that night and placed me on suicide watch. The next day, I was taken to county jail to await transport, and here I met tough, burly women who had already been to prison. They tried to school and prepare me, and also helped me in every gentle way they could as I endured total withdrawal. This was the first time in several years I had no drugs at all, and it was brutal. Through the chills, sweats, vomiting, skin crawling, bones aching, sleepless nights, and inability to eat, the other jail inmates stood by me. Back then, there was no such thing as a medical detoxification. When I asked for aspirin, a male orderly who distributed medication said to me, "There's only one thing I hate worse than a junkie, and that's a female junkie." I didn't ask for any more aspirin.

Before I was transported to Florence, the others advised me to mind my own business, keep my mouth shut, and not to take anything from anyone. Sound advice.

PHOTOS

1. With my mom and my godmother, Aunt Mary, at my baptism.
2. A sibling photo with my brothers taken in the late 1950s.
3. I felt happy as a child and I loved playing with my brothers.
4. We had a lot of fun together as a family.
5. I cherish this portrait of my mom. This was taken around the time when she became pregnant with me.

6.

9.

7.

8.

10.

6. One of my elementary school photos.
7. A family photo when Harvey was part of our lives. He was such a savior to us.
8. My mom and I during the time when the beatings and molestation were our reality. We were smiling but we were trapped.
9. Me at the age of 15.
10. A family photo taken when Manny was part of our lives.

11. Being hippies with my best friend, Marci.

12. Steve, my first love.

13. Dink, my prison mentor.

14. Hanging out in the prison yard with Linda and Judi in 1976.

15. Hanging out with Jackie in prison.

16.

19.

17.

18.

20.

16. A holiday photo taken of me in 1975, while I was in prison.
17. My first Christmas in prison.
18. The first "professional" photo after being released from prison in 1981.
19. Being stylish in New York in 1983.
20. My biological father, Eddy Sassoon.

21. Hanging out in Munich, Germany, in 1982 with my cousin Uvall and aunt Raina.
22. My girlfriend in Germany, Ruth, from Ebenhausen.
23. With mom and Ruth in Tucson after Ruth came to the states.
24. Joanne and I at Amity in 1987.
25. Joanne and I were so happy together.

26.

27.

28.

26. Isn't she lovely? Joanne, my loving wife and partner for 25 years.
27. Joanne with first grandson, Eric, right after he was born.
28. A family photo taken in the early 1990s with my mom, brothers, and sister.

29. Joanne, my beautiful bride, on our wedding day.
30. Walking down the aisle with my mom.
31. Joanne walking down the aisle with her son, Paul.
32. At our wedding exchanging our vows.

33. Our ring ceremony.
34. Hooray! We are married!
35. Cutting our cake on our special day.
36. With my partner, Liz, enjoying a vacation together in 2014.

PART THREE

BIG POND, LITTLE FISH

CHAPTER 17
Life Outside

1980. February 28. After four years and ten months of incarceration, I was released back into a world I knew nothing about. Frank, the program manager of Casa de Vida, picked me up in Eloy at the Greyhound Bus depot, a run-down building that used to be a gas station with a grungy café next to it. Armed with my high school diploma and Associate's Degree, I was ready to tackle life and the world.

Three years earlier, I had convinced a home girl from prison, Betty, to parole to Casa de Vida. She knew they had done right by me, especially when those Christmas boxes came each year. I found out she had married Jim, who had also gone through the program. They were both clean (or so I thought) and had a baby boy named Doug. Jim and Betty were in love, seemed content and into recovery, so I thought I might give it a shot.

Frank let me skip Phases I and II, and put me in Phase III of the program, which meant I was eligible to work immediately. Jim hired me to work as his dry wall apprentice, lying on my behalf to the foreman that I had experience. Then he put me through a rigorous on-the-job training regimen. He had been doing drywall for years and was as good as they get at his trade. Jim made it clear that until I proved myself, I was his runner.

It was the hardest work I'd ever done, carrying fifty-pound boxes of mud up two or three flights of stairs, especially when the sweltering Arizona summer arrived. I wasn't allowed to actually tape for the first month. "Until you develop some muscles, you can't tape," Jim said.

Once I got used to the job, I liked it because I could lose myself in the purely physical labor. I didn't have to think about anything complicated or dwell on the memories of prison and my past life. A few weeks into it, though, I realized Jim was using after all. He was doctor shopping for Dilaudid for chronic back pain. His pain was real, but the supply of pharmaceuticals he was getting was far more than what he needed. Betty didn't know he was using.

When I found out about it, Jim asked me, "Hey, you wanna get paid with Dilaudid for part of your check this week?"

I had done Dilaudid before, and knew it was basically synthetic heroin. "Sure, that would be great," was my answer. Every Friday thereafter, part of my pay was in Dilaudid. Even though I was in the program, I had already begun using pot, drinking, and shooting heroin occasionally. Drugs were, quite simply, ingrained in my being, and my mentality hadn't changed much since prison. I still wanted to put my lies over on whomever I could and get away with as much as possible.

The program at Casa de Vida was like many others around in the early 1980s, a Therapeutic Community derived from the Synanon treatment model established in the late 1950s. Most of the clients were heroin addicts. Unlike today, the prevailing attitude about drug treatment (outside Alcoholics Anonymous and Narcotics Anonymous) was that if you were a heroin addict, some substance use, such as smoking marijuana, didn't "count" as a slip in sobriety. Drinking alcohol definitely didn't constitute using. Thus, most of the program's upper level staff—all of whom professed to be in recovery—were at least drinking and smoking pot. These attitudes and practices caused many to relapse and die. But in my mind at the time, their behavior justified my own use of drugs.

A month after I paroled, while I was living in an aftercare facility, one of my home girls, Brenda, sent me a birthday card with two pills taped to it. I assumed they were four-milligram Dilaudids (the strongest dosage) and proceeded to shoot them. Within seconds, I found out that they'd actually been orange sunshine LSD, which was the same color and size as Dilaudid. What a shock, expecting opiates and getting LSD coursing through my bloodstream!

Somehow I was lucid enough to call another of my home girls, Bon, the one I had met while she was mopping the floor years earlier on my third day in prison and whom I'd sworn I wanted nothing to do with at the time. Once I was out of prison, I had found her because she and her laid-back husband, Billy, were dealing heroin. I wanted her to stay with me until I came down from the LSD.

"Bon, I fuckin' think I just shot some acid. Can you come now? I think I'm gonna die."

"I'll be right there," she said, and rushed over.

Without her, I doubt I would have returned to reality or sanity, perhaps even life. But once again, what should have been a wake-up call to stop doing drugs wasn't.

***

By my standards, the first year out of prison was productive. I couldn't go back to nursing because of my conviction, so eventually I quit working for Jim, got a job as a night monitor in a juvenile shelter program, and started school in August. I used mainly on weekends. I thought I could pull off living a paradoxical life, and actually did for a long time. Before this, drugs had been my number one priority. Now, I convinced myself, they were secondary to school, work, and the pursuit of more acceptable, legal activities. I was carrying twelve units at the University of Arizona, majoring in journalism, and working sixty hours a week. I got a second job on campus as assistant to the Dean of Education in, of all places, the Department of Rehabilitation. I was such a smart addict; I managed to outsmart even myself (to my own detriment).

One thing I was sure about. I wanted to stay out of prison, but I was clueless what that meant in practical terms. Now I had two jobs, and goals. Nevertheless, I had gotten away with drugs and crime for years before I got caught, and even though I'd paid a tremendous price—five years in prison and the rape of my body and soul—I truly believed there had to be a way to accomplish things and still get high. The sick, addicted part of my brain was alive and well, and dangerously justified. It would be years before I would learn that using was an external manifestation of much deeper problems. But at this point, the issues weren't even accessible to my consciousness. Deeply buried pain drove me like an invisible, metastasizing cancer coursing through my broken life. I wasn't aware that I lacked the strength at that point to face this much agony. Drugs were the easier path.

My heart, too, was breaking. Five months after I was released from prison, just when Diana was due to parole, she found someone else. She and her new lover assaulted a correctional officer and attempted an escape. Five more years were added to her term. Sadly, I realized her words and promises had been empty and meaningless and that she was institutionalized. She had been in and out of prison, mostly in, her whole life. That fact, combined with my determined, albeit naïve and misguided plan to stay out, meant I had to make a painful but necessary choice. With that choice, I lost her.

Life outside was strange. I felt I belonged everywhere and nowhere. I was and continue to be grateful for certain freedoms, such as the ability to pee whenever I want, eat what I like, watch the sunset, and be outside at night. Before prison, I had taken so much for granted. But even though being confined made me appreciate those freedoms, it would take me a couple years on the outside to feel as if they were truly mine again. In the meantime, it was as though the outside world had lived while I was confined and was still living all around me, but just beyond my reach. Everything seemed so vast, and I didn't know how to make myself fit back in. Prison had been so much easier. Then, painfully, I would consider that perhaps I belonged there. Maybe Warden Poole had been right. Maybe I could not survive as a little fish in this big pond.

Eventually, I learned to adapt, out of sheer desire to survive. Everyone I met in my new arenas of school and work had little, if any, knowledge of where I had been. Professors encouraged me, and my boss rewarded my hard work. Receiving affirmation like this was also foreign, yet very intoxicating. I began to hope, even dream, of a new life path.

The more I learned in school, however, the more curious and at the same time pessimistic I became about the world. Ignorance truly is bliss! At twenty-eight, I was seeing things around me differently or for the very first time. Trying to adjust to traffic sounds, crowds, malls, and language outside the jargon of drug addicts and convicts was intimidating and frustrating. Prison life enticed, called to, and haunted me, which made it sensible, in my mind, to shoot more dope. In the end I found that proficiency in the art of living a structured life does not always serve one well. Even with my newfound interests, abilities, and goals, I was falling into my own abyss, again. More slowly this time, but deeper. In prison, I had built more walls to add to the literal walls that surrounded me, or I had fortified ones already there. The first one probably went up at age two or three, to protect me in my crib from the pillows held over my face by Jeff, my mother's second husband, who couldn't tolerate my crying.

I used to think only convicts and junkies truly saw behind the walls, but even they only got glimpses. There were brief moments where I could see all the fractured pieces of me: the downward-spiraling junkie, the honor student, the family disappointment, the lesbian, the lost one. I wasn't solely any one of those pieces, nor consistently all of them combined. I was being born some days, dying on others, and on some days, just static within that opiate-induced, pathetic state of nothingness. I told myself the same old lie. As long as I'm not strung out, it's okay.

I managed, for the first three or four years out, to hold on. I worked, had a 3.8 grade point average, earned scholarships, and teamed with a group of male ex-cons in a Scared Straight-type program. We went to middle schools to talk to kids about the pitfalls and consequences of doing drugs and crime. I volunteered at the university's Women's Center, where I began to meet women who were socially conscious and involved, orchestrating public events and concerts. From them, I received support in my struggle to "come out" in the free world. These were real gay women, not daddies or bull dykes. I found a bit of relief in them and slept with quite a few.

But still I had the sense that I didn't truly fit in anywhere.

CHAPTER 18
My Father: Gone

My father's money made it easy to sustain the duplicitous life I was leading. In August 1980, six months after I paroled, he came to see me at my mother's house, where I sometimes went to visit if I wasn't too loaded. This was only the third time I had met him. We were cautious, distant, and perplexed by each other—still basically strangers. Nevertheless, he was decent, gentle, and generous considering that his long-lost daughter was an ex-con on parole and a junkie.

This time, I sensed urgency in him. Not far into our conversation, he told me that he had another daughter he had never met. Handing me a 1958 adoption file from Los Angeles, he said in his broken English, "I've been trying for years to find her, but it's very difficult to do from Europe. Maybe it would be easier for you."

He also said to me, "When you are allowed to leave the US, you can come to Munich and work with me in the jeans shop."

He knew I had five years of parole, during which time I was not permitted to leave the country. A bit later, he remarked somewhat randomly that Germany was too cold for him and he was considering a move to a warmer climate.

This was to be the last time I saw my father. He bought me a three-quarter-ton Chevy pick-up and from then on, sent me money every time I asked for it.

***

One Friday a few months after my father's visit, I got a Western Union cablegram from Munich. What was this? I had never gotten a cablegram from anywhere! It said, "Eddy died. Come to Munich." It was signed, "Raina."

I called my parole agent that day. She had me report to her office with the cablegram to confirm its validity, and wrote me an emergency travel pass to go to Germany with explicit instructions to report to her once a week by phone how long I would be out of the country.

By Monday, I was on a plane to Germany arranged by other relatives from Los Angeles, none of whom I'd ever known existed. My international flight was booked to depart from L.A., so on my way out, I would have the opportunity to meet Aunt Sophie—my father's youngest sister—whom he had actually brought with him on one of his two prison visits. Sergeant Singh hadn't allowed her into the visiting room, so I had only gotten a glance of her through two thick, glass doors as he was leaving. I would also meet Sophie's two daughters, my cousins. Another cousin, Sonny, also from L.A., had left for Munich ahead of me.

I spent the night before the flight to L.A. shooting coke with this old guy named Wendell, a Vietnam vet who was harmless but scary if you didn't know him. Bone thin, weathered, and disheveled, he still had an old-school toughness about him. Besides that, he always had the best cocaine in town. After eight hours of shooting coke topped off with some heroin, I raced through the airport and barely made the flight with one change of clothes, a few toiletries, and my glasses. I hated my glasses, but had taken my contact lenses out to shoot dope and forgotten to pack them.

Aunt Sophie picked me up at the airport, and I spent that night and the next day at her house in Beverly Hills. It looked like a mansion, from my point of reference. Several cousins who had heard about me came by to meet me. Their reactions to me ranged from cautious, skeptical, and seemingly judgmental, to warm and welcoming. Of everyone, Aunt Sophie was the friendliest. The family in Los Angeles owned some sort of stereo outlet warehouse. Sitting among them, I felt as though I was surrounded by foreigners, not just because of their Middle Eastern accents and dark features, but because of their obvious affluence. As I sat at the breakfast table the morning after my flight, ravenous from my cocaine hangover, I was served a full gourmet breakfast by servants. The cocaine hadn't worn off until the wee hours of the morning, even though I had shot the heroin. After only a few hours of sleep, I was left in that somewhat numb, spacey frame of mind so familiar to me after using drugs, and everything going on around me seemed like something I was watching from outside my body. My thoughts were scattered. This can't be happening. Where am I, who am I, who are these people?

Sophie's daughter took me to airport to catch the flight to Munich. That was my first transcontinental flight—sixteen hours long—and my first time being on a plane big enough to walk around. My Aunt Raina and Uncle Joel and their two sons, Oval and Urich, met me at the airport. I would stay a month in Munich with them until I left for Bat Yam, just outside Tel Aviv, where my father had a Mediterranean vacation beach flat. Raina was short and heavy-set, with a sad-looking face. Very talkative and excitable, she hugged me warmly as soon as she saw me, and then burst out in broken English, "Oh my God, you look just like Eddy. We're so happy to meet you!"

Uncle Joel, stocky like Raina, was much calmer than his wife. He had the look of someone life-worn and tired. I didn't imagine he ever talked much, as Raina seemed to talk enough for both of them. Oval and Urich were in their late teens, nice looking, very polite, and somewhat quiet, and both were students at the university. Urich was considering the military.

With her high-strung temperament, Aunt Raina bubbled over with all kinds of information about my father, including the circumstances of his death. According to his death certificate, he had died from asthma, although no autopsy had been done. Autopsies and embalming are contrary to Jewish law, because they are viewed as desecration of the body. Jewish law dictates that burials take place as soon as possible, preferably within twenty-four hours of death. By the time I got to Munich, my father's body was already in Israel and buried.

Raina told me about the women who had been in his life. "He liked them young, blond, and beautiful," she said. His current wife, now a widow, was eighteen, and he had been putting her through law school. Her name was Ingrid, and she and her family were German. Her father had been an officer in the Nazi regime. It was obvious that Raina hated Ingrid. Raina had been the one who found my father's body, at his home alone and lying naked on the couch. She had already come to her own conclusions about the cause of death.

"Ingrid killed him, I know it! He was only fifty-eight."

Raina was also who demanded my father's body be sent to Israel for burial. "My brother will be buried like a Jew, in Israel. I don't care what Ingrid wants," she spat out.

I learned that before my father's deceased body had been removed from the flat and buried the day before in Israel, someone had taken the Rolex watch and two-carat diamond ring Raina swore he had been wearing when she found him. Also missing were Persian carpets and the keys to his 1969 Sports Mercedes convertible. He had two safes, one at home and one at the bank. Both had been emptied the day after he died. According to Raina, only Ingrid had access to them. In addition, despite a lengthy search, no will could be found anywhere.

"She stole the will and took the carpets, the Mercedes, the ring, and the watch. I'm sure of it," Raina said.

No one will ever know for sure.

Once I met and got to know Ingrid, I certainly didn't believe she was a murderess or that she had taken any of the missing assets. Greedy perhaps, but not murderous. She and I got along fine. My family hated her, and the fact that I was cordial with her fired everyone up even further. By the end of two weeks, I found myself in the middle of an estate dispute involving assets spread over four countries, Germany, Israel, Luxembourg, and the US. Surrounding me were people still living World War II or still working through it and spewing hate and accusations at each other.

My cousin Sonny from L.A. had arrived in Munich three days before I did. He was twenty-two and I was told he was my father's favorite nephew and protégé.

When I was introduced to Sonny—who was sporting a full-length mink coat at the time—he said to me, "I'm looking out for your interests." Lowering his voice, he added, "For the amount of money involved, someone in Ingrid's family could hire a Turk to kill you, you know."

Raina confirmed, "Sonny has already hired attorneys for you, one in Tel Aviv and one in Munich. You are going to inherit a lot of money."

Uncle Joel and Aunt Raina were part of the beginning of a wild journey: being involved in an international inheritance case, meeting and dealing with family I had never known, and traveling to places I never imagined I would go. The whole situation was astounding to me. Here I was, this gutter-hype junkie, lesbian, and ex-convict from a state in the US no one in Germany had even heard of, now the estranged, re-surfacing daughter and surely unwelcome complication for this wealthy Jewish family. I didn't know what to make of them, or any of it. I was sure I was dreaming, but just as certain I didn't want to wake up.

Raina filled me with fascinating stories of my father and my Jewish family.

"Your father's side of the family is like two families, some very rich and some very poor. Many of them survived the Holocaust, including Joel, your grandfather, and your oldest aunt in Tel Aviv," she revealed.

According to my aunt, I had family all over the world, including Israel, Italy, Germany, Holland, the US, and Luxembourg. She and Joel had worked side-by-side with my father for eight years and were half owners of the jeans store in Munich. For three weeks, I went to the shop every day with them. Raina was the stereotypical Jewish martyr, full of drama, guilt, and sorrow. Not a day passed that she didn't cry, and her favorite topic seemed to be how she and Joel were the ones who had stood by my father more than anyone else and that no one appreciated all she had done for him.

I finally met one of the attorneys, who, like Sonny, claimed he was looking out for my interests. According to him, my father had a half-million dollars in cash and assets, and I would be entitled to between half and three-quarters, maybe even all of it, depending on which country's laws applied to the estate. There was no mention or record of his other long-lost daughter, and I wondered if Eddy had told anyone she existed. The accounting of my father's assets was ex-tremely complicated, because he had been a Jew with a Dutch pass-port, residing in Germany, and had married Ingrid in Las Vegas. In the end, it took two years of legal proceedings to locate all his assets and determine which country's inheritance laws governed the estate.

But the legal complexities didn't matter much to me. I was still in shock that I was getting anything and that my father had meant it when he said I would inherit some portion of his estate.

While the family went on talking and fighting about the money, In-grid and I did not. We actually liked each other. A full-figured, stun-ning, platinum blond with blue eyes, she possessed one of those faces a person could stare at all day. She was clever and a breath of fresh air amid all the bickering relatives.

One day, she and I were packing some things at my father's flat. Her parents were there and she started to pack some bottles of liquor.

Her father said to her in German, "If the seal is broken, don't pack it. It might be poison."

I was curious. "What did he say?" When she translated, we both began laughing hysterically. It struck both of us so funny, we didn't know why and we knew it was no laughing matter, but it did.

Then Uncle Joel called the flat to check on me. "Who is there with you?" he asked.

"Ingrid and her mother and father," I replied. Upon hearing that, and learning I was alone with them, he came rushing over with Raina to rescue me from those "terrible and dangerous" Germans.

***

I assimilated easily into the Europeans' love of travel, finding Bavaria to be so magical a place. Every Sunday, Joel took the family on trips into the Bavarian and Austrian countryside to visit enchanted castles buried in the deep, rich forests, to museums steeped in the region's history, and to tiny villages where the buildings were works of art in themselves. I hadn't done any drugs for three weeks, and this, no doubt, enhanced the wonder of seeing Europe. We went to Berchtesgaden, where Hitler's Eagle's Nest home was located. I didn't know many details about the Holocaust then, but this village of Berchtesgaden was so beautiful that words cannot describe it. Ironically, though, it was a strange juxtaposition of tremendous splendor and unthinkable evil, as it was in this village that Hitler had laid plans for the Final Solution.

Throughout the legal proceedings concerning my father's estate, the attorney in Munich gave me spending money. I started sending money to my mother and promised I would buy her a house when I returned. Ingrid and I were already dividing some of my father's belongings between us, and I shipped certain of these things to my mother.

In April 1982, I went to Bat Yam to see my father's flat for the first time. Bat Yam (a name meaning daughter of the sea) is a small suburb ten minutes south of Tel Aviv. I flew alone from Munich, and it took three hours to get through airport security because of the lingering aftermath of an incident on September 5, 1972, that had come to be known as the Munich Massacre, during which a terrorist group known as Black September had infiltrated the Olympic village in Munich and taken eleven Israeli athletes as hostages. Airport personnel checked cameras and lighters, escorted me to a tiny curtained booth, searched me, and interrogated me about whether I had been given any papers or messages to take to Israel. To me, this intrusion seemed familiar, even normal. The questioning, the searches, and the suspicions were just like those in prison.

It was a charter flight, and the plane was so old that water was leaking through the windows from outside. My mind was filled with terrifying visions of the plane nose-diving into the Mediterranean below us. Everyone applauded when we landed safely, which I later witnessed as a common practice in some countries. We deplaned and were greeted by soldiers with M-16s, waiting at the bottom of the small stairs from the plane's exit to the "holy ground." My pulse had just settled down from surviving the plane ride, but now it was racing again with the certainty that they were waiting to arrest me. Paranoia is a hard habit to break. These soldiers, it turned out, patrolled the whole city, as well as the beaches, another common occurrence.

When I arrived in Tel Aviv, I had to find a cab driver who could read the address of the flat in Bat Yam, which was written in English; most of them knew only Hebrew. The flat was on the fourth floor of a huge, relatively new apartment complex. It had two bedrooms and two balconies: one balcony overlooked the Mediterranean, and the other had a view of the city. It was fully furnished, and exquisitely so. Raina had told me that various family members used it throughout the years as a vacation home. After I unpacked, I ventured out to buy some food. I had changed $200 US to shekels, which turned out to be such a huge wad of bills that I really needed a purse. Instead, I stuffed the bills in my pockets. After I bought groceries, someone on the street managed to steal the rest of the money. I didn't realize it until I got back to the flat, and I was amazed that someone could have reached into my pocket without my knowing it. Suddenly, I became keenly aware that I was a stranger in a strange land, and caution would be advisable.

The local news that day also delivered an unsettling report—which I learned in my short trip outside—that the bones of a twelve-year-old

Denise Sassoon

girl who had been missing for three days had washed up onshore as the gruesome contents of several plastic bags. No crime so heinous had ever happened there, and the faces of the people showed heavy sadness, panic, and suspicion. Children were being escorted everywhere and forbidden to play outside.

After only my first day there, Israel already seemed like a dangerous place, with soldiers, crime, strange customs, and the murder of this young girl. Nevertheless, I'd already seen worse in the US, so it was fairly easy for me to put aside my fears and enjoy the excitement of this adventure. Any residual withdrawal symptoms from my previous drug use were gone by now, because I had been doing drugs only sporadically. I felt good, energetic, and invigorated. Maybe I didn't need drugs in my life at all, ever again.

I stayed a month in Bat Yam and met more family members: Moesha, my father's father; Mida, his oldest sister; and several cousins and uncles. My grandfather Moesha lived in a meager, one-room shack with a dirt floor in Tel Aviv, and someone came in two or three times a week to shop, clean, and cook for him. Although he didn't speak much English, he seemed happy to meet me. And even though he was eighty-six, I could still detect a mischievous gleam in his eyes. Of all the family I met in Bat Yam, he and Mida were the two I liked the best. Mida, who had a tattoo on her forearm, a fading yet unmistakable reminder of her time in a Nazi concentration camp, informed me that my grandfather was actually a millionaire who owned entire streets in Tel Aviv. As I got to know different family members, I realized how many of them were waiting for Moesha to die in hopes of inheriting some of his vast fortune. I met and befriended a cousin named Noya, a young Jewish girl with piercing brown eyes and jet-black hair. She even scored some hashish for me from an attorney she knew, and we partied together several times.

I met the second attorney who had been hired for me. He was handling the estate in Israel. Supposedly, Israeli law dictated that I would get 100 percent of any assets there, and thus would inherit the flat and everything in it. Meeting with this attorney took up much of the time I spent there. The rest of the time I spent just walking around the city in complete amazement.

My time in Israel was rich and enlightening, especially for someone who had never traveled. In awe, I watched horse-drawn carriages driven

132

by old men and heard the wailing of Hebrew chants, songs, and sales pitches for their goods. I visited Jaffa in old Tel Aviv, which dated back to the time of Noah's Ark, and saw Mount Ararat, where the ark came to rest as the floods receded. Noya took me to Jerusalem to see the gold dome and the Wailing Wall. There was a sense of family in Israel that was unlike anything I had ever seen in the States. Children and elders were revered and protected, and most families were intact and had fathers, mothers, and extended family all living under the same roof or very close by. The other striking thing about Europe and Israel was how fresh World War II still was in the minds, hearts, eyes, and conversations of the people in both countries. In Germany, there seemed a real sense of guilt among some youth for the crimes against humanity their ancestors had committed, even though they personally had had no part in it. In Israel, it was most noticeable in the eyes of the elders, a sadness perhaps of all who were lost.

When my time in Bat Yam drew to a close, I went back to Munich for a week and then returned home to the States.

CHAPTER 19
Back Home

Flying over the Swiss Alps and watching the sun drop into the ocean, I pondered my life and this dramatic turn of events. I now had over $8,000 and a possible quarter million coming soon, in addition to my father's watch and ring, both of which had been recovered by the attorneys. I thought about all my newly discovered family members and the unforgettable places I had visited in my travels. My head was filled with fears, hopes, and ideas that had not been there before. It felt surreal, like a miracle or something. But the grip of reality was there, in the form of craving drugs. I hadn't used heroin since I had left Tucson, nearly two months before, but the closer I got to Tucson, the more that familiar urge overwhelmed my consciousness.

While I was overseas, my neighbor in Tucson, Ann, a very close friend and previous lover, had been maintaining my house, rent, and other routine affairs. "Mother" to seven cats, Ann was a mellow little pothead, a very shy, soft-spoken gal. Needles scared her, so I suspect she was wary of me. Ann wasn't what one would label an addict, plenty of people, even among the lesbian and university communities in the 1980s, were addicted primarily to alcohol and cocaine. It always seemed comical to me that there was and is such prejudice among drug addicts, especially nonintravenous versus intravenous addicts. As if the manner in which one ingested drugs made some difference morally!

By the time I landed in Los Angeles, I was in a trance as if on automatic pilot, but something told me to call Michelle, an old high school friend, and say, "I'm landing in an hour. Can you go cop, and pick me up? We're going to party!"

Michelle and I had been casual lovers over the years. At this time, she was married and eight months pregnant with her second son. She was an on-and-off drug user and one of a few select people in my secret heroin circle, who were a group apart from my other, "functioning" life.

Michelle didn't let me down, showing up at the airport with all the must-haves for getting wasted. But when I finally got home, a surprise awaited me. Ann and my friends outside the orbit of my drug world had organized a welcome home party. Everyone I knew had heard of the story and the passing of my wealthy, long-lost father. When Michelle and I walked in the door to a chorus of noisy greetings, we were so loaded that we just stood there, nodding out. Instantly, all those faces in my living room took on looks of shock and disappointment. For them, my homecoming had become sad and hard to witness. For me, it was a glazed-over event barely noticed through the numbness of drugs. Somewhere deep inside, though, I was also upset that after such an astounding trip, my first priority had been to score heroin.

I resumed my life in Tucson—work, school, and dope. The big difference now was that I had money. Michelle and I became inseparable, heroin our common bond, and because I had the dope, we slept together more often. Although I knew better, I told myself she loved me and would finally leave her husband for me. It never happened. We just conveniently used each other.

***

I didn't get it, didn't get why I couldn't stop shooting dope. Why didn't I have the will power? I knew when I got high enough, everything was numb, still, and quiet, a respite from the constant torment of self-hatred. It was a no-win, ugly cycle: I hated myself every time I got off, and I got off when I hated myself. The nagging conflict, relentless and exhausting, of believing there was some part of me strong enough to stop that could overcome, and yet not doing it. I suppressed the urge to ask friends, family, anyone, to close their arms around me and help. Now, everyone who knew me could tell when I was using. I had long since stopped asking anyone to understand or be patient with me. During my first two years out of prison, my parole agent referred me to various therapists, through whom I began to understand myself better, understand why I had opted to check out of life at eleven years old or younger. But my efforts at therapy were, at best, half-hearted and inconsistent.

I dreamed of loving anyone as much as I had loved, and still loved, Diana. She, too, had heard of my recent windfall. We were writing and I was putting money on her books. She would someday be out of prison, and I deluded myself with dreams of picking up where we had left off. But Michelle was there, and at that point, the closest person in my life. For fifteen years, she and I had been going around, in, and out of each other's lives. We were using daily, but I was still an honor student working two jobs and doing speaking engagements. The people in my other life, mostly women, were artists, activists, professors, and students. I envied them their ability to drink, use cocaine, or smoke pot occasionally and maintain balance. I was using heroin daily for months at a time, although I still wasn't getting terribly sick when I didn't have it. Reaching the level of tolerance that renders a junkie sick without the drug takes a while. Of course, this made it that much easier to justify. Again, I told myself, at least I'm not strung out.

One of the therapists I saw, a brilliant and inspiring woman, seemed as baffled as I was about my slow descent. One month, two articles in different publications, *Rolling Stone* and *Science Digest*, suggested that because heroin has been proven to stimulate and increase production of the body's natural endorphins, when one stopped using it, the body craved a return to homeostasis, at least. The articles said that it takes the body years to balance itself again, pointing to this as the cause of addiction to, withdrawal from, and repeated relapse on heroin. After studying the information, I couldn't wait to tell my therapist how happy I was that my addiction was not my fault, but rather a physiological problem involving my endorphins. In truth, this was just another rationalization for more using.

My mother had divorced Manny during my third year in prison, but he still controlled her life, as is so common for women who have suffered years of abuse. She had not yet gained the strength to stand up to him while he continued to maintain dominance over many aspects of her life: whom she spent time with, how she spent her money, and how she raised my younger sister. He still called her names and criticized her every move. Because of this, I didn't visit home very often. That, plus I didn't like anyone in my family seeing me loaded. My brothers were both married, building their own families, and Jeanette was a teenager. The fact that Manny was her father made me anxious and scared for her when she went to spend time at his house. I didn't know if he was raping or beating her, and I dared not ask. I didn't yet know how to open up about such horrible atrocities.

When I had promised my mother I would buy her a house, my intentions had been sincere. But intention amounted to only that. Instead, I let her watch me put the inheritance into my arms. My limited awareness made it impossible for me to realize the profound impact that family has on a person, so I certainly couldn't see how hurt, angry, and disappointed I was in mine. I didn't know that on some level I was getting back at my mother for not protecting me as a child, but hurting myself in so doing. In my random sessions of therapy, I was just beginning to learn that all this had to be worked out. At the same time, however, I found myself feeling twinges of guilt about how I was hurting so many people in my life, especially my family. I know that until she died my mother still perhaps feared those phone calls in the middle of the night, which might bring news of my death lying on a bathroom floor with a spike in my arm. I could see her fears for me in her face, especially her eyes. I knew that every person in my family wondered whether I was using. I didn't have a place to put all this. Outwardly, I was distant and withdrawn, yet inside I felt desperate for something more. But I had no idea how to get it.

***

In August 1981, five months after my father died, the attorney from Munich called and asked me to meet him in New York City regarding the inheritance matter. He said he would be at the Drake Hotel on Park Avenue and that he had reserved a room for me there. Still on parole, I had to get another travel pass. By luck and skill, I had not violated parole and was in good standing legally. School was out for another month and I hadn't been working much, spending most of my time hanging out with my two tightest companions, Michelle and heroin. I decided it would be a great opportunity for me to stop using dope for a few days, just in case I was strung out again (there was no way to know except to stop and see what happened). So off we went, Michelle and I, with a $20 bag of dope between us. With relief we found that we didn't become sick, hence were not strung out. We spent the week living it up, buying clothes, eating at the best restaurants, and making love. We had been clandestine lovers for so long, and it felt so liberating not to have to hide it for those few days. We saw the original works of Picasso and Rousseau and walked around Broadway and Harlem. We saw the Guggenheim and the Museum of Modern Art and went to the top of the Empire State Building. I stood there imagining my mother and father being there thirty years earlier. One day we walked a hundred blocks (which really is not that far in New York), savoring every nuance of the city.

Flying out of New York, I realized that every time I left Tucson, I was happier, freer, and less driven to shoot dope. So that must be it, I thought; Tucson is the problem. Tucson was why I shot dope, and of course, those pesky endorphins that my body stopped producing.

CHAPTER 20
Back to Europe: Ruth

Staring at a miniature cactus sitting on the kitchen windowsill at Joel and Raina's, I wondered what in the hell a cactus was doing there. I was back in Europe at the advice of my attorney, eight months after my first trip. Sitting there, I was depressed and fearful as I thought about the state my life was in, the money I was about to inherit, and of course the dope. I started to weep. I felt so alone. I knew my Hungarian Jewish Uncle Joel felt alone, too. After spending time with him and Raina, I could tell. And I could see it in his eyes. He had survived the Holocaust, but not without grave damage. I guess a great many people survive their own personal Holocausts of varying degrees. Mine was heroin, forcing me into a constant struggle to overcome the destruction of my veins, my soul, and my life, but mine was self-imposed to some extent—big difference.

At least for the moment, however, I was safe here in Germany and about to have another adventure. I decided that while I in Europe this time I would venture out more to meet other people my father had known. Eager to learn all I could about him, I asked those who had known him questions about his life.

One of his ex-girlfriends, a woman named Christa, told me, "He was very vain. So vain, he wouldn't wear glasses which he needed to drive. So he hit a cow in the middle of a country road while we were taking a Sunday drive!" Christa was a stout woman, a blond with full chubby cheeks and a wide beautiful smile whose family lived on a beautiful farm and raised horses. "He liked young women," she went on, "and he was very good-looking."

Eddy, I learned, had been in scrapes with the law and had gambled throughout his life. During his travels throughout the world, according to Raina, he had played bridge with Omar Sharif in Monte Carlo. In talking to my attorney, I heard him refer to a portion of the cash assets as "black money," income on which my father had not paid taxes. The picture I formed about him from what people were saying was that he had been kind and gentle but also playful—too playful for some—and shrewd in business, extremely shrewd. What was left behind of his life seemed to indicate that he had lived well and enjoyed life. I hoped he had. I missed him without ever knowing him. From what I could tell, we were similar in many ways, for example, in the free-spirited, optimistic, serious, yet playful and adventurous aspects of my personality.

The attorneys in Munich and Israel said it would be months before I could leave Europe because of all the legal complexities still pending. I was fine with this, elated to be away from Tucson, and looking forward to seeing so much more of glorious Europe. One night, I ventured out to a club called Frauenkneipe I had found in a LGBT directory at a tiny corner bookstore. I hadn't come out as a lesbian to my relatives, surmising it might shock, offend, repulse at worst, or at best baffle them. They were traditional "old school," of a different generation, and I told them I was going to see a friend I had met at a bookstore.

I took the U-bahn to the bar, but arrived way too early, around 5:00 p.m. There was only one other person in the bar besides the bartender, and I sat there feeling alone and awkward as those two studied me, hard. Unlike Americans, who are subtler, German people have a way of staring as if they're looking through you. I found some literature at a table, walked up to the bar, and ordered ein piltz, a beer. I drank, wrote in the journal I had kept on and off since prison, read awhile, and drank some more. Two hours and three stout beers later, a few women had wandered in. Every one of them shot that same stare at me as the first two had and then went on talking and drinking. I'll never forget that the Dexy's Midnight Runners song "Come on Eileen" was playing from a jukebox in the corner. The music, and no doubt, those few stout beers helped me just sit, watch people, and relax.

A woman came in and instantly caught my eye. She stood out in her orange and black zebra-striped pants with green suspenders, black high-top tennis shoes, and wire-rimmed glasses. Gangly looking, she had to be nearly six feet tall. The lower half of her head was shaven and the top was short and perfectly spiked. Captivated, I followed her with my eyes as she made her way to the bar, got a beer, and sat down at a table alone. Her gait and demeanor appeared confident, yet there was an uncertainty or hesitance about her. She glanced over at me a few times, and not with the stare I had gotten from so many others. I sneaked glances back toward her between my sipping and writing. I also stood out with my nappy Jewish hair, short stature, and big nose. When I ordered, it was clear to anyone in earshot that I was American. I attempted to speak the limited German I had picked up on my first trip there and in German classes in school. I had studied German since my father's first visit two years earlier when he told me that someday I would travel to Germany. Though limited, those tidbits of education were certainly coming in handy now. The night wore on. Almost everyone in the club at one point or another had sized me up, but no one approached or talked to me. I was getting buzzed and stopped writing, sat awhile, and then figured it was doubtful that I would meet any of them and that I should head home soon.

Only minutes later, the tall woman with suspenders got up as if to leave, but stopped at my table and asked, "Was sind Sie schreiben?" (What were you writing?)

I had been writing about her, describing her outfit, so I replied, "Actually, it was about you. I was describing your clothes."

When I told her that, she said, "Würden Sie bitte wenn ich Sie trat?" (Would you mind if I joined you?) And so she did.

It was delightful to talk to someone outside my family, particularly a woman and, even better, a woman in a lesbian bar. She spoke surprisingly good English and was impressed with my German. I later learned that English and Latin were required in high school for all German youth. Her name was Ruth, and she was just nineteen. I was almost thirty. We stayed until the bar closed, which in Munich was 4:00 a.m. Then we took the S-Bahn to a tiny village called Baar-Ebenhausen nestled against a ridge of a stunning mountain range. We walked a few blocks in the snow to her home, which was on the third floor of a 100-year-old Victorian home surrounded by other homes, each of them unique, grand, and breathtakingly beautiful.

Ruth lived with Heinz, an 82-year-old friend of Ruth's father. Heinz, I would come to find out, was in love with Ruth. No wonder. She was extremely bright and serious at times, curt, and refreshingly different from anyone I'd ever met. She made a huge impression on me immediately. As I got to know Heinz better over the next few months, I liked him and grew to love him. He was the most remarkable, intelligent, gracious, and unselfish individual I had ever met—and undoubtedly the most educated. It did strike me as odd, however, that he was in love with someone who could have been his granddaughter.

On our second date, Ruth and I went to a punk club called Blackout. The punk movement was raging in Germany, and it looked as though many of its most hardcore devotees came to this club. The punkers wore every color, shape, and style of hair and had multiple body piercings. They accessorized three-dimensional outfits in electric-bright colors with studded leather collars, belts, and bracelets. But the people seemed dark. Their eyes were cold and hard to read. Ruth introduced me to a young man she had dated before. A few minutes later, I looked over to see him kissing her while she kissed him back, wantonly. I didn't know her well enough to know what she was doing or why. I wasn't sure whether she was just drunk, confused, playing some kind of game, or just being mean. Maybe this was a cultural thing, or maybe I had misread our intense lovemaking and our conversation deep into that first night. At any rate, I wasn't going to be humiliated.

"Obviously, you want to be with him tonight, so I'm going to take a cab home," I said.

She followed me outside, "Please, bitte nicht! Don't leave."

"Well, who do you want to be with, him or me? You're sending some pretty mixed messages?"

She chose me, and we left together, back to Ebenhausen. All night we made love, the confusion weaving itself between our bodies. In the morning, I left her *Notes to Each Other* by Hugh Prather and took a quiet, picture-perfect ride back to Munich on the train, feeling unsure, insecure, and yet hopeful that I would see her again.

West Germany was more beautiful to me each day, and the more I saw, the more I could almost dream again about my life's possibilities, untainted by syringes full of heroin. I was discovering that my father's estate and my potential portion were substantial. Dreams of being in love, having money, traveling, perhaps opening a women's halfway house somewhere, and finally fulfilling the potential I knew was somewhere inside me grew more vivid, nearly real.

A few days after the Blackout bar scene, Ruth called me and we started seeing each other as often as we could. She was still in high school, and it was at least a half-hour train ride between Munich and Ebenhausen. In December, she invited me to move in with her while I dealt with the business of my inheritance.

I asked, "What about Heinz? You told me he's in love with you. How will it be for him? Has he even agreed to this?"

"Of course," she said. He told her he was happy I was moving in, that he liked me. I couldn't get back to Munich fast enough to let Joel and Raina know. I had been gone most nights anyway and they knew something was up, that I had met a German "friend." Without stating it explicitly, their disapproval was clear. I didn't know what they disapproved of, that she was German or that she (and I) might be gay. I didn't care. My tired, heroin-addled and worn self was falling in love with Ruth. She was like the antidote to my never-ending struggles. Suddenly, I felt young, alive, and excited.

I did want my family to meet her, though, so one night after I had moved we met for dinner and went to, of all things, a drag show. Because Joel wasn't the type to go out to bars, much less one with a drag show, Ruth and I met Raina and my two cousins for what turned into a comical, strange night. We were all drinking tequila shots. From what I did remember, we had a great time until I spent a good part of the night on the bathroom floor hugging a toilet bowl. I had a vague memory of my family insisting that I go home with them while I clung to Ruth and said, "Oh no, I'm not. I'm going with Ruth." As I said this, I planted a big kiss on her lips. Typically, when I drank, I was one of those happy drunks, never a mean or belligerent one. If the family didn't know before, they knew then that Ruth was my lover. But as stunned as they were, they remained gracious toward her and later toward Heinz.

Ruth and I spent the next day in bed recovering from the tequila poisoning of the previous night. We drank some tea, ate bread and cheese, and smoked some hash. Then we made soft, gentle, hangover love, if such a thing exists. Later that night, though, my eyes closed to see deep and vacant places. Were they my emotions? My soul? It seemed a million years ago that I had touched the soft curves near Ruth's thighs, even though it had only been that morning. Perhaps the timing was wrong, perhaps the cold climate was wrong, I didn't know. But suddenly, without knowing why and for no obvious reason, I felt tired again, so tired.

The tracks and scars on my hands and arms were healing, and living in Ebenhausen was splendid. Even though Heinz was in love with Ruth, he had accepted that he would never have more than a platonic relationship with her. He treated me as though I was family, and I started meeting his friends. During World War II, Heinz had been a historian and writer, but under Hitler's regime, he had been forbidden to write or work. I noticed that although Heinz and many of his friends were political anti-Hitler activists, while most of Ruth's friends were in or just out of high school, both groups were so much more educated about culture and history than their American counterparts despite their age differences. I was also struck by the obsession among the German youth to go to America. Almost all of them had this longing and dream, and the more I saw of Europe, the less I understood why.

Many Europeans spent their leisure time traveling. Just as my aunt and uncle had gone on mini excursions every Sunday, so did Heinz, Ruth, and now me. We went to villages and cities and drove through the countryside in Bavaria and Austria. Heinz could tell us the history of and stories about every tiny village or town we passed.

When there was inheritance business, I stayed in Munich. One night, Ruth called while I was in Munich to arrange a spot for us to meet later, and from there take the train back to Ebenhausen. She said, "Go to Marienplatz and look for a monument called Mariensaule." At 7:00 p.m., as I was waiting for her, a grand building (which was the courthouse, I learned later) came alive with music and chimes. Elegant stone figurines set high upon it began to dance. It was like a giant music box in the sky. I actually started spilling tears, overwhelmed by the beauty of it. Every day brought more of these sights, which fed my aesthetically starved soul. It was a far cry from prison, to say the least.

One morning in Ebenhausen, I was sitting near a window in Heinz's library as Aretha Franklin sang in the background on American FM radio. "We were sitting on a wall of happiness, a wall of love, he fell, I fell..." Diana came to my mind as I gazed outside toward the mountains. Two hundred years before, I mused, someone else had sat by this same window, dreaming of a lover they had touched, loved, hated, wanted, or lost. The mountains, majestic and snow-covered, resembled the Catalina Mountain range in Tucson, and with that resemblance, all the memories of past loves touched me, almost as if they were right there, in that room.

Suddenly, a news flash interrupted my reverie, something about a convicted murderer in Huntsville, Texas, who had been executed that morning by lethal injection. He was the first, the report went on, to be executed using "this new, more humane way for the state to kill convicts." Nevertheless, observers of the execution saw the prisoner wheeze and jerk about in pain for several minutes. The broadcast was a rude intrusion of ugly reality that didn't belong here in this beautiful house, this beautiful land, this beautiful life.

Later, Ruth and I went walking in the snow and I asked her, "What's the name of the mountain range facing us?" She said it was the Alps. I nearly fainted. Could this be so? Here I was, holding a walking stick, in the company of a woman of whom I grew fonder every day, out for a morning walk at the foot of the Alps. I had not used cocaine, heroin, or needles in weeks. Ruth and I smoked hash or pot and drank on occasion, but this was the longest period of time in at least 17 years that I had not used hard drugs. Yes, it was so, and at that moment I couldn't imagine anything better. We walked for miles. The sun one so seldom saw in Germany was out that day, reflecting rainbows on the snow. We walked to a baroque church along the river Paar, and later got stoned and went for a ride in the countryside. I was marveling at the beauty of a pond I spotted in a small farming village, until Ruth told me this pond was where the dead cats of the village were thrown! We laughed until we cried. Even a pond filled with dead, decaying cats was full of hilarity and enchantment.

One night, I was awakened from a sound sleep by a nightmare. Earlier that day, I had found a small section of the library in Munich that had books in English and picked up William Burroughs's book *Junkie*. I'd read the whole thing in one sitting. It felt as if Burroughs had written it for me. I could so closely relate to his poignant, graphically detailed life, described as only a heroin addict could. In my dream, a thin, black man was holding me hostage. It took place in Tucson, and my brothers were there. I was sitting on a ragged couch watching television, while my mother sat near me in a big, overstuffed, red chair. The thin man stood outside the front door on a porch that wasn't familiar. He turned toward where I sat, and he seemed safe enough to invite in. But once inside, he brought out a gun. He was robbing us, I think, but then he started playing Russian roulette with the gun pointed at my head. The room began to fill with people, some of whom I knew and some I didn't. The man and I exchanged words, but I only remember him saying to me, oddly, "Hey, how you doin'?" I didn't answer. I was crying. More people came in. Each person who came in sensed danger, but didn't do anything to help. I wasn't sure if they couldn't or wouldn't. The man seemed spooked by something and suddenly grabbed Jonathan around the neck and said he was going to kill him. Then he declared that the only way he wouldn't was if my mother would sell me to him. My mother agreed to it, and he let Jonathan go, telling him to run as fast as he could. As Jonathan started running, the man shot him in the back. The dream ended there.

I tried to make sense of this horrible and vivid nightmare. Perhaps Burroughs's images had taken me back to the old times: the rapes in 1974, my mother's empty arms, and heroin. He wrote that heroin is a way of life whether one is using or not. He said it is always there in our cells and in our spines, that when we do it after having been without it for some time, it is comparable to meeting an old lover and knowing you will go to bed together. I cringed at the old cliché once a junkie, always a junkie. At my core, I knew that upon my return to Tucson, whenever that would be, the whole of my being would cry out for heroin, and I would answer and hate myself for it. Again.

I fought with myself as I sat in the Konditerrei, watching the rain and attempting to order breakfast with eggs that came nearly raw in a special dish made for them, part of the gross fruhstuck (big breakfast), and ein dunkel oder ein piltz (a light or dark beer). Beer was served all hours of the day in Germany. People often ordered a beer before their coffee at breakfast. I was reading letters from home, missing my friends and family, while knowing home was the worst place for me to be. The letters kept me up-to-date on the news. My brothers, Nate and Jonathan, were married. My baby sister was in junior high school. My mother was anxiously awaiting my return so we could look for the house I had promised to buy her. As I read, I felt a wave of frustration with the attorneys and the time-consuming complications of settling my father's estate. I had such mixed emotions, homesick and sick about home.

A letter from Michelle, however, reminded me that this storybook trip was just that, a storybook trip, and that heroin could, and probably would, destroy it all. Destroy me. It was nearly Christmas, and my thirtieth birthday was fast approaching. Although it was my third year out of prison, I still felt like an alien with no clue about what to do next or who I was, where I fit in this vast universe too complex for me to comprehend at that moment. I was struck by the two-sidedness of the life I led—my wondrous European travels with two of the greatest people I'd ever met, and my ugly life in Tucson, burdened with a potentially fatal heroin habit. On American FM in the Konditerrei, Linda Ronstadt came on singing an old familiar song, "Different Drum." She was a home-grown Tucson girl who started out with a band called the Stone Ponies in the 1960s. At this moment, home was so distant, as though it didn't exist, like a shadow in a vague and dark dream. I thought of all the dying I didn't do when I was away from there, and how strongly I walked on paths that led away, so far away, from there.

Just then, an intrusive radio news flash broke in. Americans were falling dead from taking aspirin that had been laced with poison.

I wrote home to let my family and friends know I would not be there for Christmas and spent most of the next couple of months at meetings in lawyer's offices, listening to everyone toss my deceased father's name around and fight over his estate. They all spoke German and I wasn't fluent enough to understand everything. I just wanted it over so I could figure out what to do next to get on with my life. Perhaps I'd make it better, perhaps not, but I was tired of waiting. Everyone in the meetings—the attorneys, my family, Ingrid—was interested in getting as much as they could of his estate. I wasn't consumed or concerned with that, because the whole circumstance of my father's leaving me anything seemed like a mistake or a miracle. To be sure, regardless of how the estate would settle, it was more money than I had ever dreamt of having. But after each of those legal meetings, I found it harder to be in the meetings.

Heinz, Ruth, and I went to Wurtzburg for the Christmas holiday to meet an old friend of Heinz's named Petra. She was a divorced mother of three children: Andrea, Stefan, and Jacob. Heinz was excited, almost like a child himself, about the upcoming visit, evident from the gleam in his eyes and ear-to-ear smile he wore beneath his little Italian cap.

He had known Petra since she was a child. The trip turned out to be exceptional, starting with our drive to the city. On the way, we passed a number of villages scattered throughout the countryside, like picturesque settings plucked from an old-world Christmas art book. When we reached Wurtzburg, we followed a narrow cobblestone street to a building that did not look like a house. It was situated between two businesses. Heinz rang a buzzer, and we made our way down a dimly lit hallway to an austere, gray stairwell that spiraled upward to a series of doors on the second floor. When Petra appeared, my first thought was of Heidi, the fictional little girl who lived with her grandfather in the Swiss Alps, only twenty years older. With a dress that gathered flatteringly at her waist, blond hair worn long and loose, and fresh, young face, Petra looked to be somewhere in her forties. She hugged and greeted us warmly; it seemed clear that this was a home flowing with love.

Christmas Eve was brilliant. Just before midnight, Petra gracefully and ceremoniously lit the candles on the Christmas tree using a sparkler. Then she lit the tops of steins filled with seven different liquors, poured each of us a cup, and made a Christmas toast, "To happiness and life." Her children's eyes were wide and bright with anticipation of what would come after the toast—opening the gifts! Petra handed me a package wrapped with a string held together by a small slice of wood with a hole in it. The note said "I love you" in Japanese. Inside were three books. Her thoughtfulness, the intricacy with which she had wrapped it, and her attention to detail made this small gift one of the most touching of any I'd ever received. At midnight, we donned coats, hats, scarves, and gloves and walked across a field of snow under the brightness of a full moon to midnight mass. As we neared the ornate church, we heard a choir singing in Latin. The sound drifted through the chilly winter air, beckoning us to come inside. I had never been to a Catholic mass and although I didn't understand Latin, it was a truly spiritual moment. After the service, all the way back to Petra's house, I cried tears of true joy and wonder with the world, with my life, and with this Christmas Eve.

While in Wurtzburg, Heinz introduced us to many more of his friends, all of whom were scholars, writers, poets, and artists. Everyplace he took Ruth and me, we were given gifts, modest but touching gestures of humanity and goodness. I felt honored to meet all of these people. While riding in the car between stops, Ruth and I sometimes smoked pot. Then we'd go into restaurants giggling uncontrollably while strangers stared at us curiously. Heinz would get a contact high and giggle with us. Sometimes we'd all wind up laughing out loud.

Heinz, Ruth, and I we were such an odd, happy trio.

CHAPTER 21
The Tax Man

Not long after our return to Ebenhausen, my attorney called to say that I would soon be hearing from a tax official assigned to work on the case, and the cash assets of the inheritance would be released that day.

"Your assets," he told me, "particularly the jeans shop in Munich and the flat in Bat Yam, could be tied up for years before they are cleared." He added, "If you want to return to the States, you are free to do so. There is no more business you can do here for the now."

I was both ecstatic and distraught. My life still felt suspended. By my humble standards and welfare upbringing, I was now wealthy. I had found a home and fallen in love with Ruth (and Heinz, too). Sometimes in the morning after she and I had made love or had just awakened, Heinz cooked us feasts with what I thought were odd combinations, such as eggs, trout, and lasagna accompanied by Earl Grey tea, but no matter the combinations, they were always scrumptious. He would wheel the food into our room on a serving cart, with a wink and a light in his eyes. He loved seeing Ruth in love. I considered getting a work or school visa to stay in Europe. Even though I was still on parole, I was pretty sure I could tell my parole agent that the case was not yet settled, buying myself a few more months. Eventually, though, I would have to return to Tucson to buy my mother the house I had promised. A rough plan formed in my mind. I'd get my mom settled, pay my taxes, get off parole, and then move to Europe.

I went to the Bayerischen Bank to withdraw the money now at my disposal. I took Ruth with me, and then we got a room at the best hotel in Munich—the Bayerischen Hoff—and celebrated. We went on a shopping spree, bought the best champagne there was, got massages, and ordered room service. The next morning we went back home, got Heinz, and then went to visit the home of some friends, Cookie, Helga, and Christa. Meeting any of his friends was always a treat; they were diverse, interesting, smart, and so open-minded. Cookie was Helga's husband, and Christa was lover to both of them. It felt so alive and comfortable at their house. Bavaria was so much more sexually liberated than America. We ate ice cream and chestnuts and drank much good beer. A few nights later, Heinz took us to a small dinner at a house where two women lived. He had known them since the war and they had been lovers for fifty years.

Life was full of lovely new experiences and people, but each passing day made the thought of going back to Tucson harder. Ruth and I decided to rent a little Volkswagen Golf and drive to Italy. Why we rented such a small car given the money at my disposal was a weird choice, but oh the times, laughter, and adventures we had in that tiny car! I noticed that European people vacation often, much different from the one or two weeks that people in America take annually. People traveled to Venice, Verona, Greece, and Rome, Greece being one of the favorites. We stayed in hostels in three different countries. In Verona, I saw the courtyard that inspired Shakespeare's scene from *Romeo and Juliet*, when Romeo calls to Juliet from below as she stands above him in the velvety-green, moss-covered balcony. Legend has it that this house belonged to the Capulets and that good fortune will come to those who rub the right breast of the bronze statue of Juliet in the courtyard. My other discoveries in Italy included the oldest outdoor opera house in the world, the statue of Dante at the Uffizi in Florence, and St. Mark's Square. When we first arrived in Venice, we drove back and forth over the Ponte Della Costituzione four times trying to find our hostel. Still lost, we finally asked a cab driver, "How do we get into the city?" Wearily he told us, as he had probably told a hundred other tourists that day, "You cannot drive to Venice. You must hire a water taxi to get there." Venice was unforgettable.

Aside from my family, I didn't miss anyone or anything about Tucson because now I had a home here. I had a lover, friends, and so much more to see, void of heroin no less. But alas, I also had a parole agent I was mandated to call every week and report on the progress of the inheritance case. She pointedly reminded me, "If you lie to me, you do know that I can violate your parole and send you back to prison. As soon as your legal matters conclude, you have to return to Tucson." But I wasn't too worried about it. Most of the documents regarding the estate were in German. I couldn't see her going to the trouble of getting them translated just to figure out whether I stayed longer than necessary.

The case settled not long after we returned from Italy. Everything except the flat in Bat Yam and the shop in Munich was divided in half between Ingrid and me. We both received around $100,000 in cash, after the attorneys were paid. The attorneys got a third of the $500,000 estate. The flat in Bat Yam would be mine when it cleared Israeli law, and I sold my half of the jeans shop in Munich to Joel and Raina. Although I hadn't understood most of the proceedings, documents, or intricacies of the case, the attorney in Munich was paid, his job was done, and he said that I needed to retain the attorney in Tel Aviv to obtain a clear title to the flat. Also, there were still physical assets consisting of Persian carpets, the Mercedes, and a flat full of antique furniture. My family convinced me to sell some of them, saying that shipping them to the States would be extremely costly. The cash assets were wired to an account in Tucson.

That winter in Bavaria was unseasonably sunny and warm, but like the native Germans, I was happy the day it snowed again. And on that day it snowed heavily. Gazing out my favorite window in Ebenhausen, I once again contemplated the ironies in my life. My father's appearance out of nowhere at the most opportune of times. I was at the bottom, broke and in prison. His looking for and finding me had led to my inheriting half of an estate overseen by the laws of four countries, meeting family members I had never known existed, and having the opportunity to touch history, culture, and art in the company of wise and educated people. I felt an urgency to capture it in words, to write it all down. This would be an upbeat, different kind of story, the extreme opposite of what I had written in prison. But when I tried to capture in words what I had seen, felt, wanted, and feared, they seemed so trite. I wrote anyway.

I had no idea what to do with the amount of money I now had. Of course, everyone around me was full of advice about what to do. I knew I wanted to buy my mother a house and get myself a decent vehicle, but beyond that, I had no clue. I was confused and terrified not only of the heroin and cocaine fantasies I still had, but also of my more noble plans to do something worthwhile, perhaps make a real difference, with the money. I feared failure and success on even terms.

I spent a few more weeks in Ebenhausen feasting on meals prepared by Heinz, making love to Ruth, writing, reading voraciously, and dreading the thought of leaving. Ruth loved reading, too, and on snowy days we often sat in front of a small fire and read to each other the words of Hugh Prather, Erica Jong, and Norman Mailer. While reading *Belly of the Beast*, we thought perhaps Mailer should write a story of an ex-con that had a happier conclusion, one in which his main character and protégé paroles, doesn't stab a waiter, and ends up staying out of prison. We laughingly planned to call or write him. I shared with Ruth my love affair with heroin, my prison experience, and the ugly sides of me. She seemed intrigued by my stories of a culture and experiences so foreign to hers. I was intrigued by her lack of shock or fear.

Not long after New Year's, I went to Lufthansa to inquire about my return trip and buy a ticket for Ruth to join me in America later. She had to finish her last year of high school. At the airport, there was no record of my arrival, and my return ticket was good for a year. For a fleeting moment, I thought it was a sign that I wasn't supposed to leave, but I proceeded with the reservations. I would leave in two weeks and Ruth would follow a couple of months later. I couldn't stand the thought of leaving, but Ruth, like so many European youth, dreamed of seeing America, and knowing that she would get to fulfill that dream took a little of the sting out. I still didn't get it. Their country, their lives, their customs were so rich in history, art, and culture. After what I had seen traveling, my opinion of the US had changed, not in a positive way. My homeland seemed repressive, shallow, and deficient in everything that abounded in Europe.

Until I left, I tried to savor every vivid detail of Munich, Ebenhausen, the snow, the Alps, and Heinz, all of it, every day an adventure. I went to Englisher Garten Park in Munich one day while Ruth was in school, after having smoked some amazing homegrown weed that Ann had mailed from Tucson. I watched people feeding popcorn to ducks, reminiscent of another park in another place. Sitting there and pondering, I realized that more than anything, the things I had encountered here and in Israel had given me a broader perspective than I'd ever had, a genuine appreciation and reverence for history and humanity. I would never forget the people I'd met on this trip and would miss them greatly, especially Heinz.

Earlier that morning, Heinz and I had been together drinking Turkish coffee from special Turkish coffee cups, while he filled me in on the history of coffee. We had talked about Ruth, life, and love.

"Heinz, I adore and I love her. I hope you know that. She's filled a three-year void of darkness," I had said to him. "I plan to take good care of her." Sparing Heinz all the dirty, shameful details of my drug history, I had touched on this aspect of my life only superficially. He knew that Ruth and I smoked pot and hashish.

"She dreams of going to America, and I want to take her there," I continued.

Heinz had replied, "I know, and this will be such an adventure for her, one that she will never forget." Then, looking at me intently, quietly, and almost in a whisper, he thanked me for loving her.

The music playing in the background included Lou Reed's "Heroin" and some songs from Willfried, a German rock artist I had grown to love even though I didn't understand most of his lyrics. After telling Heinz a little about my life in Tucson, I thanked him for giving me Verona, Venige, Wurzburg, Salzburg, his friends Petra, Helga, and Cookie, and most of all his home. We laughed together as we imagined Ruth in America, with her six-foot self, her chartreuse socks, orange pants, pullovers, high-top tennis shoes, odd haircut, and wire-rimmed glasses. I loved all these things about her.

***

A friend wrote me to beware of fortune huntresses. I wrote her back that I did not think they came in the form of beautiful women, but rather attorneys, banks, tax officials, and probably a select few of my relatives. My anxiety about returning to Tucson had crept up on me, and I was showing signs of stress. I had worked my way up to smoking two packs of cigarettes a day while trying to plan my life, or at least the next few months. I craved more strength, more direction, and more stability in my emotions, so much so that the image of and desire for a needle in my arm intruded upon my thoughts, even though I was still here in Europe. The drug fantasies seemed so out of place, but there they were. Once I was off parole, I wanted to travel the world, do something grand and meaningful. But the yearning to shoot a big speedball (heroin and cocaine together in one shot) and fade back into the abyss overshadowed my respectable intentions and took my breath away.

CHAPTER 22
Sun Going Down

After eight astounding months in Europe, I returned to Tucson. It only took a few days back home for the whole thing to seem like a dream from which I'd been wakened against my will. Deciding to pursue my Bachelor's Degree, I went back to the University of Arizona, and my old boss hired me back. I changed majors three times, finally focusing on journalism, English literature, and women's studies. I began reading more voraciously than ever before. Meeting Ruth, Heinz, and all those extraordinary people in Germany and Israel had fired up my desire to search, to learn, and to become wiser.

Having money was a welcome relief after living most of my life so deprived of it. I was occasionally shooting dope, but noticed that for brief intervals when I was doing things that motivated, challenged, and intrigued me, I didn't seem to need the dope as much. Smoking pot was harmless to me; it was the means by which I could enhance my vivid imagination, and indeed it worked. Most of my better writing came when I was high on pot. I lived alone at first and then tried having roommates, but none of them lasted very long. The only exclusive or intimate relationship I had was with Michelle, and that one was primarily about the dope.

In my view then, everything came down to choice: whether to hurt or not, shoot dope or not, laugh, cry, write, and even breathe sometimes. When I shot dope, I was disgusted with myself for making that choice. It would be years before I would learn that after a point, addiction does not involve choice. I was as yet unaware that we are all driven by our conscious and unconscious experiences. We are driven largely by pain, past and present, from such things as the cruelty of our childhood, the loss of loved ones, the rape of our bodies, or the struggle of just plain living.

We all have some times in our lives when we do something so out of character that we surprise even ourselves. Around this time, I experienced just such a moment, and it was one I'll not forget. It seemed everyone I ever knew had heard of my windfall, and people from my past seemed to be crawling out of the woodwork to tell me how much they had missed me and how much they wanted to see me. One morning an old connection showed up at my house.

"Hey, can you loan me some money?" he asked.

"No, I don't have it," I replied. At this, he became belligerent and started screaming obscenities at me. I stared at him, feeling my anger building.

"You fucking stingy bitch. I heard about your long-lost father, your trips to Europe. I know you have money, plenty of it! You don't remember all those times I fronted you dope?" All the while, he slobbered into his scraggly, brown beard, spewing out his disgusting words in breath that stank of stale beer. He looked like a possessed madman.

I said, "No, I don't remember, and please fucking leave now."

He persisted. "Do you want your jaw moved to the other side of your face?"

I wasn't prone to anger, at least outward anger. The few times I had lost my temper or been violent were the result of extreme provocation and were few and far between. But on this particular morning, I was so infuriated with this unwelcome visitor that I punched him in the face. It shocked both of us! Never in my life had I hit anyone, except to defend myself. I tried later to understand what chord in me he had struck, but I couldn't figure it out. Perhaps it was that, once again, I had friends or lovers only because I had money, much like what happened in prison after my father came along. It was as if people thought they had something coming because I had shared some dope with them once or twice years before. Or maybe punching him was just a demonstration of that ever-present coexistence of dark and light inside me finally loosed.

There were days that I felt as though the walls of prison still surrounded me. They became the sky. Prison was inside of me now, I figured, and even the sky wasn't big enough to get me out. The very air felt as if it was crushing me. I took a writing class in which the professor required everyone to journal at least two pages every day. This actually turned out to be a relief. Once writing became an assignment, I had to find the discipline to do it. It was hard at first. I was unable to write when I did heroin. Words bled and made no sense, reminding me of how alone and guilty I felt when I shot dope. My mandatory journal begged, pleaded, screamed at me to stop using. The more I wrote about not using, the more I used.

By the time Ruth arrived in America, I was on the verge of a habit again, but not enough to prevent us from driving up the California coast. I had bought a Ford 150 half-ton pick-up with a camper, and we took off as soon as summer break came. For two months, I was free again with my young, innocent, sweet lover, and from heroin. We stopped in Vegas on the way. It was my first time there, and even though I had over $100,000, we played quarter slots and were elated to win 400 quarters. Years later, I would discover that, like my father, luck was on my side in gambling.

Driving along the ocean was so majestic. I had only seen the ocean twice before, during that horrific summer in Key West when I was sixteen, working on the shrimp boats with my brothers to support our family, and again in the 1970s when Marci and I had hitchhiked to San Diego to see the Allman Brothers. I remember we ate a bunch of acid that weekend, met three blond, tan, surfer hunks who had a house at Sunset Cliffs, and tripped with them for three days after the concert.

Ruth and I took our time and stopped when we felt like it. We saw every beautiful mission and beach from San Diego to San Francisco. In San Francisco, we met some radical feminist lesbians and a phenomenal black woman, a blues and jazz singer named Gwen Avery. We went to the largest Gay Pride march in the world and saw Holly Near and Linda Tillary concerts in the Castro. We went tubing naked on the Russian River outside Guerneville. Ruth marveled at the newness of America as much as I had marveled at the oldness of Europe.

When I thought of us going back to Tucson, the day grew dark before night came. Just before the trip, I had thrown all my syringes and dirty spoons away and flushed the little stash of dope I had, a first for me. I told myself that this act was my way of standing up and taking charge. The weeks passed, Ruth came, all was well, and quitting dope seemed feasible. I even set my anniversary date for being "clean" from heroin. And yet, during those last two hours of the trip back home, all I could think of was calling Michelle. It seemed inevitable, and so it was. The second day we were home, I called Michelle to say, "Go cop some dope and come over, but you can't say anything to Ruth. She has no idea that I'm doing this, so just play it off." She brought it over, I introduced her to Ruth, and we took turns going into the bathroom to fix, while the other kept Ruth distracted. This was the way Michelle and I devised to hide our dirty and, eventually, daily little ritual.

Soon, and right before Ruth's eyes, I changed. Ruth had never met or been exposed to a heroin addict, and although she didn't know specifically what was going on, she knew something was different. Gradually, I lost interest in music, making love, going out, eating—basically, in living life. Ruth loved America and my friends, but my habit forged a wall around me and between us. I was still on break from school, and the plan was that she would return to Europe when the new semester began. Instead, only a month after the California trip, I told her the truth.

"I'm using again, and every time Michelle comes by, she brings dope. That's why she comes so often." I will never forget the hurt and lost look in Ruth's blue eyes, which filled with tears of sadness for us both.

"Can't you stop, for us?" she pleaded.

"I can't promise you anything," I told her truthfully. "I wish I could, but it's got a hold on me."

We mutually decided, for her benefit, to change her airline ticket so she would return to Germany sooner, and within a week. The day she left was devastating. The reality that I was consciously choosing heroin over Ruth was almost, but not completely, unbearable. I had flashes of Diana then, too. Did I love Ruth, or would I ever be able to love anyone as much as I had loved Diana? I didn't know, and by the time we reached the airport, neither of us could talk. We cried and held onto each other those last moments, as if doing so would change the harsh reality. Over the following weeks, I tried to comfort myself with the thought that I had protected her from more hurt with my decision, but the guilt that I had brought any hurt to this young, innocent, full of life girl/woman was ever present too.

I was a junior and still earning nearly a 4.0 grade average. At thirty-three years old, I felt out of place much of the time in a world full of twenty-year-old students. But I reveled in this world of learning. I couldn't get enough. With most of the required credits completed while I was in prison, I was well on my way to the Bachelor's Degree. My journal chronicled my struggles during this period: the ever-present fight against my drug habit, the strangeness of being one of the oldest students on campus, the challenge of trying to fit myself into the free world outside prison, and the rigors of keeping up with my classes. I discovered that the more I learned, the more intensely I felt everything. Thus, I developed a true understanding of the expression "ignorance is bliss."

Ruth and I were in contact by letters and a phone call on the 24th of every month, the anniversary of the date we had met. But over time, she and Europe were fading into memories. I began dating a woman named Lynn, who was an artist, astrologist, and activist in the women's movement. Lynn was the only lover I've ever known who had an open relationship. Her main lover was also an artist, but they both slept with other people. It worked for them, and for a while, it worked for me too. I thought it was great that a couple was that secure and trusting of one another.

I was very attracted to Lynn, and she and I had a standing date every weekend to go hiking. The hikes we took were amazing, and each week we challenged ourselves to walk higher and farther. Madera, Pima, and Sabino canyons all had trails that wound through landscapes that changed as one hiked from the lower typical brown dirt and cacti to the higher flowing creeks, pools between giant rock formations, green trees, and moss-covered forests. I loved being in nature and being witness to its wonders. It was serene, a place to reflect and be at peace, even if for a brief time.

Lynn introduced me to more women, radical women who organized events such as camping trips, concerts, marches, and art gallery openings. We went on campouts with other women, ate mushrooms, smoked pot, and drank tequila. I surprised myself by finding out I could sleep on the damp ground even knowing that all kinds of bugs crept underneath me. Lynn taught me that Mount Lemmon, a peak in the breathtaking Santa Catalina mountain range near Tucson, was named for botanist Sarah Lemmon. In 1881, Native American guides led her to the top on mules and by foot. She climbed the entire nine thousand feet to the top and was the first female in the country to accomplish such a feat.

In addition, Lynn taught me about the lesbian struggle, insisting that it was our right to be angry with men. All men! I had my own personal reasons for being angry with men, but didn't agree with her dismissal of a whole group or gender as unworthy. I thought it hypocrisy to fight oppression, yet oppress others, and to rail against stereotyping and then practice it against another group. The women's movement, relatively speaking, was still young; it wasn't until 1986 that the Supreme Court ruled that sexual harassment was a form of illegal discrimination in the workplace. Women discovered their anger.

All my friends knew of my "past" struggles with heroin, but none knew it raged on inside me before their very eyes. They were unaware of the double life I led, only seeing the student, the activist, the would-be writer, the ex-con who had "made it." They were oblivious to my secret rituals: the shared dirty needles, the ooze of red as the needle registered, my blood mixing with the heroin and cocaine, and the feeling of dope coursing through my veins, enshrouding me in numb separation from the world. A part of me wanted to believe I could stop. I was intelligent and compassionate, and I dreamed of writing something that someone, someday, would want to read. I always had this feeling that what I wrote and what I had survived mattered, that something should come of it.

I discovered that I had little use or tolerance for small talk. Sitting in a waffle house at breakfast listening to waitresses talk about their boyfriends, parents, money, school, and someone's C-section, I thought how unimportant most talk is, like white noise. Not that I was above it, just apart from it, apart from life really. Distancing myself like this was a trait in me that I both deplored and embraced. The only times I felt truly at ease were those brief and rare moments I spent with someone who had been a convict with me. School, work, and activism didn't leave much time for a social life, but I was still loyal to the code, the one that automatically deemed anyone I did time with as a true friend. Yet I also had to keep my distance from them because I was determined not to go back to prison, and nearly everyone I knew went back or never made it out. As comforting as my home girls were, I feared their influence over me. Deep down, too, I knew most of them weren't and never had been true friends. I had been out three years and was just beginning to feel as though it might be possible for me to stay out.

I was obsessive about school and maintaining perfect grades. For example, when I had reading to do, I first highlighted the main points, typed them out (before people had personal computers), highlighted the typed version, and kept this with me everywhere to stare at, memorize, and learn. The further along I got in my coursework, the more consumed I became. But I didn't notice, or chose not to notice, that I was using more often. Weekend binges didn't end on Sunday, but reached into Monday and sometimes Tuesday. Family and many of my friends were seeing my all-too-familiar, gradual descent away from them. Occasionally, I could get four or five clean days in a row and found myself delighted by this tenuous bit of control, because it meant I wasn't strung out. When I did manage a few days, it felt as if my soul slowly started to creep out of my scarred veins, but very, very carefully for fear of hoping too much. My good grades and success at work made it easy to run game on myself. Shit, if I could get A's and shoot dope at the same time, I must be really slick. In some twisted way, I prided myself on pulling off this double life.

CHAPTER 23
Freedom's Just Another Word

One of my roommates had three cats, and at night they ran the streets and howled and screamed into the cold darkness of the desert. It terrified me. Their screams became my screams—screams of insanity and confusion. I still had a fair amount of the estate left, making it easy to keep using. The flat in Bat Yam was not yet in my name. It would be soon, and then I planned to sell it. I hadn't bought the house for my mother, even though I could have with the money I had left. But I put it off, telling myself I had plenty of time. In the meantime, I avoided my mother and family, only seeing them on occasion.

Much of my writing during this time was about the conflict and dichotomy of my life and of me, filled always with the unanswerable question of why I kept losing the heroin battle. No matter how fast I tried to run away from it, it was winning. I could not figure out why. On the one hand, I was so inspired, motivated, and delighted with school— reading and interpreting *Gulliver's Travels* and *Beowulf* for English literature and writing short stories that got accolades from fellow students and professors—but in between classes, I was racing to the connection and then back to school in time to fix inside the bathroom nearest the next class. My money afforded me the option of doing speedballs, that sweet mix of heroin and cocaine in the same shot. The cocaine amplified the chaos.

When we were asked to read our work out loud in class, I used this as a venue to make bold, angry, and what I'd hoped were thought-provoking statements. Once we had an assignment to interpret the views of St. Paul of Corinth and Aristotle on women, and to my dismay, both these scholars believed women should remain silent. Their words ate away at me. In fact, I was outraged! I knew my writing, as in prison, had become my vehicle and release. My life now was helping me understand that prison is much more figurative than literal. Time is just time; we are all doing it. As Janis Joplin so aptly sang, "Freedom's just another word for nuthin' left to lose." Prisons became life, and cities became prisons, especially this city. I felt so trapped.

When I didn't shoot dope, everything in my world was more vivid. A song, a poem, even a newscast could inspire an eloquent essay about life. Hearing Peter, Paul, and Mary singing "Leaving on a Jet Plane" resulted in something I titled "Romanticism Is Hell," a lament on lost love. Though I'd had lovers since prison, I never stopped loving Diana, and we were still writing to each other. I had even gotten approval to visit her and smuggled dope into the prison a few times. There were dreams again—mine—of our long-awaited life together when she paroled, and promises—hers—of enduring love. But I wondered about her, as I did about almost everyone who had reappeared in my life, how much I deluded myself about her intentions.

For this reason, I relished the anonymity of a big university campus, a campus full of odd and wonderful characters that I wrote about on Sunday mornings in the front yard while smoking joints and studying German. I sifted through old journals, notebooks, and wooden boxes full of paper and tiny dead scorpions to collect and organize my scattered writings, out of which characters were born. These characters defied the powers, the bureaucracies, the parole officers, and declared themselves free of the illusions of justice and logic. They also looked for comfort, but did not find it. In these characters, I could reconcile how love made sense in a world filled with cruelty, shrieking cats, bugs, hairy legs, Armantha, and nappy hair.

On my third anniversary of being out of prison, I felt very lonely, not so much for physical intimacy but more for intellectual or emotional connection. Barely managing more days clean than loaded, I knew this was why the loneliness prevailed. Even after three years in the free world, I remained watchful, skeptical, and paranoid—still on the outside looking in. Life touched me, but I couldn't reach far enough to touch it back, and it was maddening. When I wasn't using, the window of my soul got washed and I dared to believe the dreams that heroin hid from me. When I wasn't using, my sinuses cleared up, my period resumed, my eyes dilated to the right size, and the abscesses on my arms began to heal.

The awkwardness I had with people on an intimate level, perhaps because of my convict ways, was causing every roommate I found to move out. They all said it wasn't personal, but I knew it was. I knew I had that uncanny ability to distance myself so that others felt unnoticed and unimportant. It wasn't intentional, nor did I like it, but as keenly aware as I was of the effect it had on those around me, I couldn't (or perhaps didn't want to) change it.

Coming out, and the segment of the lesbian community of which I was a part, disillusioned me. I detected double standards, which I didn't like. One day at school, I noticed a guy singing as he skipped down the street. I was sitting on the soft, green grass at one of my favorite spots on campus studying for a math test. Seeing that he had caught my eye, he walked over and asked me for directions. He introduced himself as Bertrand and said that he had just arrived from France only to find that the phone number and address of the people he had planned to visit did not exist. He said someone else told him there was a shelter or travel center close by. I got a good feeling from him, and he seemed safe enough, not to mention extremely good looking and so charming. Because my roommate was in Florida visiting her mother for one month, on a whim, I offered to let him stay at my house until he figured something out. He wound up staying nearly a month, and we became good friends. Ironically, he was also into heroin and had with him a half-ounce of China White, which I had heard of but never done. It was nearly pure heroin and the best I'd ever had. We stayed in touch and remained friends for years.

When my roommate returned and discovered I had let Bertrand stay at the house, she and almost every lesbian I knew told me in no uncertain terms that I had disgraced, tainted, and soiled the house with "male energy." By inviting him in, they said, I was asking to be raped. I was completely stunned by this reaction, not only because of their lack of faith in my instincts, but even more so because of their clearly separatist attitudes and politics, neither of which I wanted to be part of. That I was gay I had no question, but I had no interest in belonging to a group that excluded others for reasons that I couldn't justify or, worse, for no reason at all aside from gender. Their prejudice toward men as a species and their broad generalizations about men confused, confounded, and disillusioned me. The attitude that being persecuted justified persecuting others was reminiscent of the inmate-versus-convict prison dynamic that I'd learned to loathe. I loved women but didn't hate men, and I was relatively sure that a number of my friends had not suffered the molestation, beatings, and brutal rapes I had endured. In an attempt to explain my actions to my roommate, I wrote her a letter and, in doing so, came to the realization that part of the reason I invited Bertrand to stay with me was fear of being in a house alone. Rationally, I knew I shouldn't be afraid to be in a house by myself at night, but the emotional scars of rape remained deep, open wounds and relentless. My phobia, I realized, was a direct result of being raped by those ski-masked men. I also recognized that this anxiety would always be within me to some degree, but even so, did not give me the right to fear or assume that all men were violent rapists!

The outlook of my circle of friends left me outside looking in with yet another group, intensifying my ongoing frustration in feeling as if I didn't fit and was thus alienated. Writing about the distancing, frustration, and fear helped, but didn't provoke any insight into how to fit. My life was filled with lovers but no relationships, letters from Ruth were dwindling to none, I was smoking too much, and another roommate was moving out. My rare moments of free time were spent with Michelle or watching the news and *Mary Hartman*. I was obsessed with Louise Lasser for a while.

***

One day while out trying to get businesses to buy ads for a Women's Center concert brochure that we were producing, I took a break and sat down on a curb on Meyer Street in one of the oldest neighborhoods in Tucson. There I sat, near the barrio, near the connection, near the parole office, in the sun, under the sky. Poor old dirty Meyer Street, poor old dirty Tucson, I thought, poor old dirty people being pursued by a Papago Indian police car that sped by just then. I started having black thoughts about the reality of who I was, who I had become—a tired, desert sun-child, junkie, ex-con, student, daughter, and lesbian— and how easily I could end my fifteen-year battle with heroin. Hadn't I already made the decision years before, after the rapes, after prison, after multiple relapses? Almost, but I'd never made it, partly because I couldn't imagine being only average, and somehow, in my mind, doing heroin, being a dope fiend prevented that. But the cost was so high. Hadn't I more than paid it? Of course I had, but there I sat, desecrated, teetering on that curb, on that emotional ledge where suicide seems more painless and sensible than life.

Speedballs weren't cheap, and my money was going fast. I still had the flat in Bat Yam and a few assets. I had very little cash on hand and was basically living on a couple hundred a month. My truck broke down, an ex-lover was moving in, and the seams holding my "selves" safely separate from each other were beginning to unravel. The evening and weekend junkie was starting to overpower the college senior who wrote short stories, crawled out from under piles of old journals, books, and German prepositions, and struggled with math that had me biting fingers where my nails had been. My writing spilled from the depths of the deepening tracks on my arms, which I stared at with such disdain through my drug-pinned eyes. I sold my truck and bought a Suzuki 500, which made it easier and quicker to cop dope in between classes. Without a doubt, things were closing in. The vehicles, the cats, the roommates, school, Michelle, Lynn, the dope, the lies I told myself.

My gut wrenched with the truth. Dope was winning, consuming everything I did, every breath I took and wreaking havoc. One morning, loaded, I slipped on a wet street. The bike and I went down hard, and I scraped my arm pretty badly. Some homeless guys in a park across the street ran over and helped me and my bike up off the wet ground. I thanked them and went on to class, oblivious to the fact that blood had seeped through my sweater and jacket. My professor excused me to go to medical and get my arm cleaned and bandaged. The next night, I stayed on campus an extra two hours for *Das Boot*, a German movie my professor had offered extra credit to his students to watch. The extra credit would move my B plus to an A. I waited a half hour in the empty modern language auditorium before someone practicing a piano on a stage near the curtain finally asked me why I was there. He then informed me the movie wasn't until the next night.

My grip on reality was loosening, and fast.

By my fourth semester in German, I was fluent enough that I started writing in German to Ruth again, to Heinz and Ingrid, and in my journal. It was elementary, but I was impressed that I could churn out two or three pages. Ruth was going through hard times with her parents after she came out as bisexual. She had finished high school and decided to take a break, hang out with friends, travel a lot, and live back at home. However, her ultra-conservative parents were appalled that she was seeing men as well as women, and threatened to disown her if she continued down that deviant path. Any words of encouragement or comfort I wrote or tried to convey on the phone seemed trite, empty, and inadequate, even though they were heartfelt. I was also guilt-ridden for what I had put her through, exposing her to the ugliness that is addiction.

After several months of being in the open relationship with Lynn, thinking I was so progressive, it began to affect my already low self-esteem. I wanted to see her one weekend, but it was Gayle's (her main lover) week. I needed her that weekend and felt deprived, which led to my having doubts about our entire relationship. There could be no spontaneity or permanence in the arrangement we had. I realized it was what it was, static, predictable, and scheduled. Lynn was another one of the many people who impacted my life deeply. Something about who she was and the way she carried herself inspired me, or forced me, to look at myself, my life, my weaknesses and strengths, and my womanhood. But on an intimate level, the hopeless romanticist in me knew there was something lacking. We were never going to evolve to another level, and I needed more than a casual, every-other-weekend lover. She had someone else to fall back on and I didn't, at least not anyone who was committed to me the way she was to Gayle.

So Lynn became another in a long line of lovers just out of my reach. I knew she cared about me, but at the same time I sensed apathy; she could do with or without me. During those lovely hikes we took, I had touched the surface of my struggles with heroin, and I'd told her enough that she began to recognize the signs of when I was loaded. The more honest I was with her, the more distant and firm she became because being loaded became the more frequent occurrence, and she finally had enough. She let me have it and let me go, saying, "You are such a wonderful woman, a great lover and writer, and I love spending time with you, but not the addict part of you. I can't hang with that."

I was still at a point in my addict brain that if I shared my struggles with anyone close to me and if they dared to have an opinion about it, I blamed and resented them for withdrawing from me to protect themselves. I thought them self-righteous. I had no clue that my compulsion to do drugs was destroying my relationships with everyone who crossed my sordid path. Lynn and I had shared long talks, deep into one another; long walks, deep into the hills and mountains; and long hours, deep into each other's bodies. After all this, she was supposed to stand behind me no matter what! I wondered how she could take what we had so lightly. Her stance and the decision she made about breaking up with me ate away at me, as did her persistence in wanting to learn the details of my propensity to use and then, upon hearing those details, rejecting me and finally opting out! My attitude epitomized the selfishness of addicts, who completely disregard how they hurt and affect everyone who loves them. Deciding she was a sanctimonious bitch for discarding me, I made her the focus of my anger and resentment. In my mind, she was symbolic of all the people in my life who had abandoned me. As she was leaving, Lynn told me to come back when I got better. I thought to myself, "Bullshit, take me as I am or don't have me. It's your loss, not mine!" I couldn't write her out of my mind.

Hell, what was the difference between addictions to women, heroin, smoking pot, and drinking or gambling, I wondered. Everyone I knew did something to escape. Inevitably, the end result of any addiction was the same: burnout, regrets, loss, and pain.

***

My German teacher, who had always intrigued me, worsened the sting of lost and unrequited love. She was very young (especially to have obtained full professorship status), blond, with an innocent face and remarkable brilliance, wisdom, and excitement in her career. She seemed wholesome, too, and quietly seductive. I enrolled in her class for six semesters. Like a love struck teenager, I was under her spell and was convinced she felt something for me. Every semester, I sat in the front row, made straight A's with the exception of one B plus, and participated willingly, uncharacteristic of me in other classes. By fourth-year German, I worked up the courage to ask for her phone number or address, anything that would ensure our continued contact outside school. She gave it to me, and we met for a few beers. When I was introduced to her tall, blond, strikingly handsome boyfriend at an Oktoberfest event at a park, it was clear that my instincts had been way off. We did remain good friends, until my impending descent. It seemed as though everyone with whom I was intimate or wanted to be intimate was unattainable. I didn't know if this was chance or if I unconsciously set it up that way to hide in the safety of my carefully constructed shell—or, perhaps more aptly, my cell. Yes, cell walls were still closed in about me, even after almost four years out of prison. Lovers couldn't see inside my cell, but they knew it was there. Consequently, they came and went, but always went, in time. When would I be free? Is anyone free? Such pressing questions, but never answers. How would the story end? With a completely rehabilitated junkie or a junkie who would keep filling her veins—perhaps not as often, but always—and hate herself for it?

Good days, bad days, more bad than good. I had always been a morning person and cherished those mornings when I got to school at dawn, early enough to behold the serenely vacant lawn against a blue sky. As students started trickling in, I would study them for a moment and wonder what their lives were like. Had any of them come from the bottom, been beaten, sexually assaulted, or held hostage by drugs?

It was nearing winter break, and there were finals, term papers, and stories to be written. I had written a third short story, but it seemed to lack the depth and creativity of my first two. It was based on a dream I had about the first of my two evil stepfathers, the one who had locked me out in the snow. The dream was vague, restless, and painful. But it wasn't a dream, was it? I could still see that baby child's face, questioning the chilly air and the locked door, looking up at the window section of the door and seeing his jet-black hair and piercing eyes spewing hatred toward me. I could only recall Jeff's face in that one moment, no others. What had happened to other memories, good or otherwise? I didn't remember my mother's face, or how she smelled or felt, until we moved west to San Antonio. I began to realize that during my youth, when we lived with Aunt Ellie, neither she nor my mom was demonstrative with any of us kids.

I urgently desired to change my lies, and my life. But those desires were always overshadowed by the nagging chatter in my head that said junkies don't change. By that time I had figured out, or gotten some insight from the various counselors, therapists, and probation/parole agents, that the overwhelming majority of people who use dope, commit crimes, and go to prison were hurt as small children and, in many cases, hurt very badly. They came from broken, abusive homes where parents and relatives didn't know better, or didn't care, and thus perpetuated the vicious cycle, resulting in another generation of people feeling bad about themselves, each other, and their world.

Now, fiction and truth were starting to blur together. There were letters, journals, finals, and term papers, all piled on top of me to meet that December 7th deadline before Christmas break. I woke up, ran back and forth across campus, drank coffee, went to bed, wrote, and tried to make myself fit in, all the while trying to rid myself of, or minimize, the paranoia that everyone around me had it together, that I was a farce. Nevertheless, I tried to be good, or better to myself, to get those around me to see all that lay beneath my weakness, that person who was kind, loving, strong, and directed. The desire to fit in meant I could attain some goals, gain some knowledge, and feel some degree of comfort in a world to which I was so unaccustomed, to progress not regress.

The notions of institutionalization and criminal justice (a definite oxymoron) both comforted and nagged at me. They constituted a system under which years render one a survivor, or not. The weak became strong and conformed, adapting to the violence, the injustice, the inconsistencies, and the little freedoms one never considers until they are gone. Some died or did life on this "installment plan," but you were screwed either way. War is hell, and prison is war. What do you do when you're all out of breath, and things eat your heart out, piece by little piece, and all you've got is one last shot to get it right again?

The short story that I finally finished provoked fifteen minutes of discussion in class. Fiction or nonfiction, is that even relevant to the emotional responses provoked? What I wrote—what I still write—is some of both, but based on a real world I live in. I hadn't found a way to dream up stories. For me as a writer, the stories were real. For the reader, I wondered, what were they? Characters were created, but hewn from my life and the lives of nearly everyone I'd ever met, merged into a vaguely comfortable space where everyone and everything made sense—a space where the sunsets shouted, alive and orange, and told me everything was good and right. Anyway, my story earned a B minus. Not too bad, but not good enough for me. Somehow I could never rid myself of the bad seed planted in my psyche by Warden Poole when she told me that I wouldn't survive in the free world. She said that outside the prison walls, I was a mere small fish in a big pond, but capable of success only as a big fish in a little pond. Those words profoundly affected me, particularly when I wasn't making it. This ex-convict thing was no easy task. Surviving five years in prison necessitated making a life for oneself to suit the culture there. Getting out meant completely reversing that process. The latter is much more daunting. It is facing life in the big fish pond.

CHAPTER 24
Melancholia

Winter setting in felt hard and cold against my heart. Love, or lust, as it were, came and went so quickly. All the relationships in my world grew shorter and more intense, with both friends and lovers. The phone didn't ring for days at a time. That human contact I longed for was fading. I recalled the winter of last year, when on an hour's notice I had boarded a plane to Germany with cocaine arms aflame from the night before. The plane and Europe had been the ideal escape from a reality I didn't want to live in. Ugliness so suddenly transformed to the beauty of family, Germany, and Israel. All the ugliness of fifteen years, twenty, maybe thirty, left behind. I couldn't recall anything as beautiful and soothing as the white Bavarian Alpine winter. At no other time of my life I had been happier. I had experienced a difference in me and in others between my first and second trips to Europe. Stern, intense, rigid German eyes full of judgment had melted to warmer and kinder ones of affection and acceptance. Europe had loaned me peace for a while. In my mind I revisited the village walls that surrounded Munich in Bavaria, vivid paintings on them telling stories, and the ancient sculptures and columns in Venice. My images of Europe were the silent, grand gestures of a long, rich history that was violent, exquisite, and sacred.

Writing for me now was like traveling, but sometimes I grew weary of the stops along the way: hard-to-navigate problems and pain, with short respites of hope, passion, and appreciation of life and nature. Time chips away at passion as it marks political holocaust created by men hungry for power and money, while the rest say and do nothing. So time is corrupt and stained with blood in little towns, villages, hamlets, and cities. Blank paper called for stories to be written, too many stories. I was a writer, but I could never quite capture the essence of what lay beneath the surface. School, however, was fast becoming the one thing I could succeed at despite the heroin, loneliness, fear, and isolation that were my constant companions.

I missed love. The anguish of its absence was keen. I longed for the chance to talk, to be myself without the real, nagging, justifiable fear of rejection. And there were other fears. I had managed to stay out of prison for nearly four years, certainly enough time to assume I might not return there. But what if this assumption turned on me in the midnight shadows of a bad dream to prove that one can never be assured of freedom? Today was tomorrow and yesterday, and it's all the same fucking day. I was certifiably agnostic, meaning, to my mind, that although there was something bigger than our mere human universe, it was ridiculously arrogant to presume that humans could define or grasp it.

I smoked cigarettes, drank coffee, and believed I could write a book about my life before I was forty. But the haunting evils of prison and heroin didn't shake loose, and I didn't think that freedom was possible. I was trapped in a web of hopelessness and helplessness, too congested with life and exhausted from the endless fight to get educated and not self-destruct. Days and weeks passed. I remained unnoticed, provoked my own isolation, and stared into the blankness of my living room. Rain. Soft thoughts and memories of convicts as they laughed, hands joined as they walked in the rain. Rainbow-skied reflections in steel prison puddles. We were, sometimes, ironically, happy. The beauty of some morning-bright sunrises tauntingly escaped my pen. I just couldn't catch the words. Countless moments occur in a day or an hour that never gain expression. Writers' minds, be they poets, journalists, classicists, must always be in pain because of all that never gets written, all the words trapped in unreachable recesses of our minds.

I wrote love in letters to Ruth from across the world. Jack Abbot said he lived in the belly of the beast. Ruth did, I did, and we all lived in different bellies. The world was the beast with which we had to contend. I was inclined to believe communication problems were not created so much by a lack of contact as by the poorness of its quality. Honest, direct communication seemed a foreign concept anymore. Shit, anyone could talk to or write anyone in the world within seconds.

MTV and the poetry of Kathleen Fraser distracted me from my anxiety over German and psychology mid-terms. Thoughts on their way to paper became rapid images of reality or fantasy in motion. That I might ever have the gift of arranging on paper those thoughts that grasped at the heart, tapped my soul, and teased my imagination became my deepest desire.

Knowing anything is vastly different from feeling it. Pain: from erratic thoughts that bordered on the edge of somewhere they had never gone. Pain: loving and then losing that love. Having truly had love makes it difficult to settle for less. I functioned at my absolute worst when I was single, and when one is single, all the couples in the world populate the bars, the movies, and the streets. It's a strange phenomenon, but always happened and always intensified the loneliness that plagued my life. Saturday was my day to write, typically, all day. I read *Mourning and Melancholia* and was sure I had both, in spades. Freud distinguished between the two by posing that mourning was a temporary, specific, and conscious state of mind and the result of a loss or the perception of a loss. Melancholia, he said, was more puzzling because it was unconscious and the result of a loss that could not be observed or articulated. He noted that in mourning, the world has grown "empty and poor." In melancholia, the ego itself becomes empty and poor. The melancholic person believes he or she is inferior, despicable. In the midst of reading this, and speculating that Freud was talking directly to me, my German professor, for whom my feelings often still festered unrequited, called. We spoke and argued laughingly about Freud and then shared our thoughts about an old Cliff Montgomery movie of Freud's life that we had both seen. Her timing couldn't have been better that night.

I entered lots of writing contests and accumulated piles of rejection letters. Perhaps *Ms. Magazine* would appreciate my fiction enough to give me the electric typewriter. What better prize for the struggling writer?

***

The house was empty. My roommates were away on a "spiritual healing" workshop. I remembered a piece I had written what seemed like decades ago. It seemed fitting. "The song of life, I have heard a million times before. But compared to infinity, a million is practically none." I'd learned to walk, to talk, almost to sleep, but my ability to communicate was lacking. I expected too much specialness that did not exist. I got hurt, tried to remove the pain, and wound up just blocking it out, using my trusty opiate anesthetic. Early on, I was forced to fear. Age three is my first recollection of real fear, so intense and perpetual. The awareness of it compelled me to want to change myself and to learn to trust. But who knew it could be so hard?

Blah, blah, blah—my sentiment on life those days—I felt like shit. I was falling into a deep, dark rut, trying to crawl out, but unable. Ignorance surely was bliss. The more I knew when I fell, the further I would fall, and then hated myself for doing it. Mechanically, it seemed easy to put things together. Emotionally, I couldn't do it. And on went life. All was always well, superficially. Few knew what was below the surface.

In a journal assignment during this time I wrote:

Living is the most serious matter to which we must attend. How sad that we don't, within this universe that caresses us. I love the bewildering Arizona sunsets, Laurie Anderson's music, and Europe. I hate my life when it stops growing, I hate child molesters and rapists, deceit, close-mindedness, and those who surrender their strength and give up hope. I want a cat that won't run off or die, a lover who meets my expectations, to write a book, to publish it, to be free of prison's haunting memories, and respect. I fear having people walk on or out on me, personal holocaust, and my mother dying. I don't want a world where bright-eyed children are snatched from beds or bicycles by hollow-eyed monsters seeping out of dark closets, nor a place where degradation, ridicule, and prejudice spread like leprosy, scarring the souls of those who simply don't fall into the excruciating drudgery of normalcy and don't want to. No to Harlequin romance, brainwashing that perpetuates and persists in keeping housewives locked in white-suburban, empty, cold bedrooms. No to twelve-year-old youths in Harlem who bow dutifully to the Mafioso-induced horrors of "boy" and "girl." No! No! To the bottomless veins that cry for the brown heroin that deceitfully suggests the richness of the earth, or as in China white, the purity of snow. Yes to those distant, foreign cities and ancient monuments that make your eyes swell with tears of wonder that spill onto cobblestone walkways. Yes to Christmas Eve, to Ruth and Petra, to those tiny, intricately carved figurines dancing on top of the Mariensaule in Marienplatz. No, yes, I don't know.

CHAPTER 25
Random Flashbacks, Journal Entries, and Memories

The air is full of trails that fly behind each thing that moves. Colors appear and disappear. Bright, vivid, distinctive yellows, oranges, and greens, but also vague, nondescript grays that project emptiness. A cheap turntable and speakers next to a perfectly stacked pile of 45-rpm records set atop a broken dresser with three of its six drawers broken. The closet remains tightly closed, because she is fearful of open closets, especially after dark. She imagines monsters will invade her bed and shove the sandman out of the window. The bedclothes are used and torn. They refuse to warm or comfort her. She crouches beneath the covers, hoping desperately for protection from that evil man lurking each night in the old green recliner in the other room. Earlier she went to Himmel Park, that hilltop love–peace–unity park of the early 1960s where all the stoners gathered to drink electric wine and dream psychedelic fantasies. Someone passed her the bottle and told her it had mescaline in it. She was supposed to be roller-skating with her boyfriend. Hours passed. Later as she and he walked home, they shared their hallucinations, one of being inside a bottle of 7-Up—sizzling, bubbly, and magic—or hearing a flute play to the sound of carbonation. Another one, millions of bright shining stars across the pitch-dark Arizona night sky were connected by pink string that swayed back and forth, gently. She kisses her sweet boyfriend goodnight and goes in the house. Her stepfather's eyes meet hers, with that all too familiar glare of anger that pierces, that warns her of what is to follow. His angry fists and pointed, black cowboy boots pummel her for being ten minutes late. Psychedelic dreams get broken as he kicks, drags, and spits on her. She takes the beating like a strong warrior, knowing tears and fear no longer work, never did, but this time, it feels as though he is turning her inside out, unfolding her life. The bubbly, magic sizzle and pink string across the sky are replaced with those acid trails behind his arms and legs as he finishes the beating. In her bedroom, no monsters escape from the closet, but the one in the recliner reclines, looks triumphant and satisfied, has another beer, and gloats. What they had told her at the park was mescaline was really STP. It was a rare hallucinogenic drug that few knew about or did. It was three or four times the strength of LSD. What she thought was going to be an eight-hour trip turned into a three-day psychedelic nightmare. The reclining monster feels, acts, and looks the same the next day. But she, she will never be the same. The night before, the beating, the acid turned a new and foreign page in the book that was her life.

**

My eyes were locked out of understanding while shadows told me which way to go. Any place but here is where love is. On that hot, August sidewalk, cars and people pass in between the ripples of rising heat waves. Every life is like this, swallowed up. Eyes locked out of understanding, hearts locked into anyplace but where love is. I can do nothing about my teeth grinding at night, like stones in the sea, about not climbing to the top of those mountains. My shadow tells me nothing. I stand and reach down into childhood crying tears that don't work, casting lovers into fantasies that don't work, and wonder why, why keep going? Letters, faces, words for poems I have never written fly into mountains I cannot ascend. The letters become shadows that hide the faces of every single person I have loved and lost in angry poems that leave a bitter taste on my silver tongue. Their faces turn somersaults in my stomach and then lie to rest, forming muscles of loss and what it means to suffer and love and write poems.

**

I remember walking along the Paar River in Munich with Ruth. I remember my new German friends and relatives telling me it was the warmest winter in eighty years and that I must have brought the desert sun with me and how that made me smile. We sat on the riverbank in short sleeves, our skin soaking up the unusual December sun, free of drugs, free of pain, full of that excitement and ecstasy only found during the "in love" beginning time in a new relationship. Talking, dreaming, planning a bright, unmarred future together while knowing we were of different countries, languages, customs, and directions, we ignored all of these and captured in that one afternoon what seemed like the beauty of forever.

***

I try using warm water to wash the needle-born scars from my hands and arms. It does not work. I try to think of ten things I like about me: my eyes and hair, sometimes my figure, my hands without my nails bitten down, my breasts, my teeth, the form and shape of my back, my clear complexion, the freckles I get on my arms and back when they get sun, my eyelashes, and my smile. I am the alternate version of Jack Abbott's *Belly of the Beast*. I am a new book. A sister of someone in prison will buy me and I will be smuggled into the isolation cell of a prison poet under her dry toast, wrapped in plastic, on a metal tray shoved though the trap door. During sleepless nights when I punish myself for the self-inflicted abuse, a blank page waits to be filled.

Religion—my first exposure was in a traditional church at five or six years old, where my mother's third husband was a minister. I thought in here were all the answers. Then during the 1960s, I was child, product, and victim, and thought there and then were all the answers. The Woodstock, baby-boomer generation was no small thing. We tumbled through time to pure, innocent, and then tragic places. I lost the cage my soul lived in.

***

Thunder is manifest in bombs that send people trembling down into cellars that will not provide them the shelter or courage they have been brainwashed to believe will keep them safe. Stones disguised as singing voices, drifting out of the solitary meadows that rage under their trodden soils, raging with tears and pain for all the victims of alleged progress and civilization, their minds troubled and questioning.

I am reminded of lost soul mates, that is, if they exist, and I am sure they do. I lost mine. My soul spins all around this cage it lives in. I'm insulated from the outside, but inside is chaos and vulnerability to the madness that swirls around me. It is cold. No one lives here.

I doubt we get that we don't get—can't understand—life. We depend on information, which controls and conditions us, and takes our money. The delusions lead to our committing physical, emotional, and intellectual suicide. Power lies within us, but we don't know it. I am aware of my power, afraid of it at times, but know it is how I survived. Women are a force, are they not? Their bodies sustain the human race and are in tune with nature's cycles: the tides, the moon, the sea, the passage of time. Women's power is so feared in some cultures that they are forced into submission, mandatory clitorectomy, stoning, and death if they dare to raise their heads or look into a man's face that is not their husband.

I wish my hair was straight; I'd color it orange and shave half of it off. My body grows fat; I grow depressed about it. When people say, "Kiss my ass," I say, "Move your nose." Being gay in a heterosexual world sucks more than one would think. I am not allowed the freedom to be myself, unhidden, uncensored.

CHAPTER 26
Surveillance

By the winter of 1986, most of the money from the inheritance was gone. I was still not fully strung out, though I was using with more frequency. Not long after I received the inheritance, a woman named Linda, whose mother had been one of my mother's best friends for over forty years, introduced me to Reese, a new connection. I had no doubt that Linda had set this meeting up, toward her gain and his. They would both reap the benefits of my dead father's estate. Reese was an older, half-black, half-Jewish man. Light-skinned, heavyset, impeccably dressed, he always wore a slick little golfer's cap. He was a contradiction in some ways. On the surface, he was gentle, soft-spoken, nearly distinguished and even fatherly man, while at the same time he was pimp to a large number of mostly young women whom he supplied with, and helped become hooked on, heroin and cocaine. Prostitution was common among women and girls as a quick viable means by which to maintain their habits.

Through Reese, I met someone named Joyce and started sleeping with her. Michelle was still around too, but by then had had the baby and quit using as much. Joyce and I were using to our hearts' content, weekly, daily, hourly, and financed by me. Most of the cash assets were gone, but I had sold the flat in Israel, and this kept me from that desperation of waking up sick from not having a morning fix. Reese came along toward the end of the inheritance, but the money from the flat still made it profitable for him to ensure my steady supply of heroin and cocaine. I started using cocaine more than I had any time before then, and the money went fast. Between classes, I was racing down the road to get that next hit of cocaine, then racing back to the university to make it to class, but not before stopping in the campus bathroom to fix some heroin to level out the intensity of the coke. If I was lucky enough to get a working vein, I made it to class on time, just as that delicious heroin rush subsided enough to go unnoticed (or so I told myself).

I soon had a $200 to $300 a day habit going. Once the money from the flat dwindled away, I resorted to my education, but of a different kind—the education I'd gotten in prison from the old-timers who'd taught me creative forms of crime. What better time to try out what I had learned than now? It was necessary. One of those crimes was forgery, "paper crimes" or, as often described by dope fiends, "running paper." The university was a prime location. I stole professors' briefcases and purses while they were teaching class. It was an easy, sure thing because most of them left their offices unlocked. Before approaching their offices, I researched class schedules so I knew who was where on campus and how long their class was. Often, they were across campus in a different building. If their personal identification number was written somewhere in their purses, which was more often the case than one might imagine, I went to the ATM and withdrew the money. Without a pin, I took their driver's license, carefully cut their photo out, replaced it with mine, laminated it, then walked right into the bank or drive-through and cashed their checks. On a good day, this scam netted up to $1,000, but usually it was around $400 or $500.

Eventually, I quit school, but kept going to the university to steal. One day I grabbed the school newspaper. Inside was a small article about a thief with a tiny grainy picture in the bottom corner of the article. It warned professors to lock their offices. I was unaware that school security had pictures of me from ATMs that I used. Clearly, the heat was on. I knew it! I felt it! I stopped going to the university and started a new scam: stealing purses out of grocery carts from women who left them unattended. Amazing how many women left their purses open in those grocery carts, and more often than not, it was a quick, easy scam to pull off. On occasion, I was chased out of the store either by the purse's owner or by the store personnel. Desperation set in. I was becoming more careless, sloppy, and obvious.

Adding to the chaos was that the crowd surrounding Joyce was rough, much rougher than any I had known. I was crossing lines I told myself I would never cross. One night, very sick, I turned a trick for two $10 bags of cocaine with an old, fat, disgusting man who sat back in an armchair while I gave him a blow job. Because he was sitting up, his floppy belly made it almost impossible to find and get to his short, thick, stupid little penis. It took only seconds to finish him off, but in those seconds, my mind went to its darkest place ever. It was worse even than those wounds that had been imprinted in my brain by the ski-masked rapists, a scarred, living painting. The person I had become, this room, this man, and this act all seemed a ghastly horror film, but it wasn't a film at all. It was I. It was not I. It was I!

Joyce and I had an agreement that any time one of us scored, we would split it, and the rough crowd Joyce hung with didn't exclude her. I found out just how rough Joyce herself was. This was the pre-cell-phone era and thus meant that whichever one of us had scored might have had to hold the bag until we could find or run into the other. Most of our time was spent running the streets, not near anything except pay phones. Many times, we didn't or couldn't wait to share the spoils of our crimes. The next morning, after I had shot both bags, I ran into her. She'd heard on the street that I had copped the night before and demanded her half. I told her I had lost it, and she proceeded to kick my ass in the middle of the street. I was trying to make it to my motorcycle to get away from her, losing one of my shoes in the process. She grabbed the tire iron out of a connection's truck that was in the driveway and was chasing me down. I started the engine on the bike and made it out of there, barely. As screwed up as I was, I had promised myself that if anyone ever hit me, which at that time had only been my stepfather and Jackie, no matter who it was, I would leave. I knew it was just a matter of time before Joyce would, and so, no more Joyce. That was the last time I saw her until I ran into her years later at a drug program we both landed in.

Soon I lost my house and began living in sleazy hotels or on the couches amid the pathetic junkies I was hanging out with, waking up sick every morning. There's an old cliché in the drug and alcohol world about "hitting bottom" before making a change. I have never agreed with this notion. I think no matter how far down one is, there is further to go. I figured the real bottom was death. But there was no question that, at that point, I had to be at some kind of bottom, particularly when that repeated image of the last trick I had turned kept flashing through my head. I remember sitting in a dirty hotel room on Miracle Mile in Tucson with Betty, my old partner from prison, and later in the free world. She and I had both sold our souls and bodies throughout the night trying to get well, then fixed inside the dingy room after we finally scored. We didn't get high, and barely got well. Sitting there at the tiny scratched, bloodstained kitchenette table, with our spoons, syringes, and ties strewn out in front of us, we both started sobbing about the state we were in. No words were spoken, only quiet and weak tears shed, falling onto the bloodstains on the table. It was an absolutely pathetic scene. Here we were, two young women held prisoner by addiction, realizing we would do anything for a fix.

Life went on like this for months—I don't know how many, but too many. Sometime in March 1986, I was picked up by the police and charged with seven counts of felony theft and forgery for all the stolen checks. They had the pictures, the paper evidence, and the culmination of six months of surveillance. If convicted on all counts, I was facing twenty-eight years back in prison, four years on each count. There I was again, in county jail, broke, busted, strung out, but still not ready to surrender. A public defender came to see me and told me what I was facing. He said I had no chance of being released on my own recognizance, and my bail was set at $5,000. I knew that meant I had to come up with ten percent of that to get released. He said that if I got out on bail, I needed to go to treatment until my case got to court. I assured him I would, all the while thinking only of getting out and copping some dope.

I called Reese, told him to get me out, and promised to give him my motorcycle in return. He bailed me out, and it was on again, the ripping and running, doing whatever it took to get well. But the faster I ran, the less I could function, or get well, or make money, or sleep or eat. The bare threads of my being were coming apart. I realized that something had to give. I wasn't so much interested in cleaning up, as tired as I was, but I knew if I didn't get to a program, twenty-eight years were hanging over my head. I had done five, and knew I could, but twenty-eight, no, not even for me. I was scared!

I looked into a program called Amity, but was told there was a waiting list and to call every day until a bed became available. I spent those weeks awaiting entrance into the program wandering the streets, stealing purses, hitchhiking to cop dope, turning tricks, and sleeping whenever or wherever I could. On days when I hit a profitable purse, I stayed in sleazy hotels, but otherwise I slept in the park. Three weeks later, Amity said I had a bed and to report to the program before 4:00 p.m. My mother drove me there and brought along my baby sister, Jeanette, who was only eight years old. Even so, on route to the program I made my mother stop at a connection so I could score and fix one last time. They sat outside in the car while I went in to cop and fix. After I fixed, I had her stop at a store so I could stock up on coffee and cigarettes before checking in. I wrote a bad check to pay for those items. A few months later, in addition to the charges I already had, they added that last check I wrote.

CHAPTER 27
Recovery

When I got to Amity, the first thing they had me do was "sit on the pew" (a wooden church bench). I was still high, which was exactly why they made me sit there to reflect upon my life and to isolate me from everyone else so not to trigger others into wanting to use. The pew was used for every new person entering the program, anyone who wanted to leave (if they didn't just sneak and run away), and anyone in some kind of trouble for violating a rule. They kept me sitting there until the next morning, when I started to get sick, and then "screened" me. The screening consisted of my being put in a room with other people in the program who were charged with determining how serious I was. Because they were all dope fiends like me, they could tell I was there only to beat my felony cases. I as much as told them so, saying things like "I can do five years standing on my head, but don't want to do twenty-eight, don't want to be in prison until I'm sixty years old." That was a mistake, as the tone of the screening suddenly changed, and they began to yell at me, call me names, and call my mother names (which was so disconcerting to me and caught me off guard). But I had been through a similar experience in 1975 at my first program, and I knew these tactics were formalities and if I just stayed put and held my tongue, I would be admitted.

As mentioned before, several programs (Therapeutic Communities, or TCs) in the 1960s and 1970s were modeled after Synanon, which was founded in 1958 and later dissolved after years of controversy and alleged criminal activity. To its credit, however, Synanon was instrumental in starting a national push to provide treatment to a population that had been regarded as hopeless, and countless individuals were helped to leave drugs and crime behind and lead productive, generous, morally correct lives. During its heyday, Synanon was called the Miracle on the Beach.

A basic premise of the TC was that to get through to addicts they had to be pushed and taken up to or beyond their emotional limits. Because feelings are numbed during active addiction, addicts were pushed to feel again, or for the first time, and this necessitated extreme measures, such as forcing clients to wear signs saying "I'm stupid" or "I'm a liar," isolating clients, and doing what were called "haircuts." There were two types of haircuts, the first being somewhat literal. All men had to shave their heads, and women had to remove all their makeup and jewelry (at Synanon, there was a short time when the women were asked to shave their heads). The purpose of this type of haircut was to remove the masks and to effect an immediate change, an external one, because internal change took more than a day. The person felt the impact of the difference as soon as the next morning when he or she awoke to find a different person in the mirror. The second type of haircut was a one-way, extremely loud conversation when someone violated a rule. While being chastised, the recipient was not allowed to say anything as the enforcer screamed obscenities and called him or her names. These verbal haircuts were issued by counselors or other clients who had been in the program longer. Designed to "get someone's attention," they often angered or hurt people and ran them out the door. Those who conformed ended up doing so out of fear of more haircuts, consequences, etc. The ones able to stand this treatment eventually became the ones to issue the haircuts. Thankfully, TCs evolved over time until by the 1990s, these tactics were no longer used.

The location of the program was beautiful, on over sixty serene acres on the East Side of Tucson, right at the foot of the stunning Catalina Mountains. The main structure on the property, called The Mansion, housed group and meeting rooms and executive staff offices. George Westinghouse III built, owned, and lived in the three-story home. He was a grandson of the man who invented air brakes for railway trains, built a business empire, and was regarded as a pioneer of the electrical industry. Through the years, the mansion had been a winter home for various Westinghouse family members, a dude ranch, a camp for juvenile offenders, and a ranch school for the daughters of the elite. It was abandoned and condemned in 1980, and Amity purchased it in 1986 to provide drug treatment.

I was in a dorm with thirty or forty women. The men were in a separate area toward the front of the property. There were about eighty people in all, as well as children. Once I was screened, accepted, and given a bed, I was assigned a "big sister" who, in theory, would orient me to the program. However, my big sister ended up flipping out, getting drunk, and leaving the next day. Another woman, Pat, took on the big sister role without being asked. In her thick New York accent, Pat told me she had lost three kids because of her addiction and related legal problems and had been in the program a few months, hoping to reunite with her children. We bonded quickly, and to this day, Pat remains one of the more important people in my life. Ours is a treasured bond.

On the second day, I was awakened at 5:00 a.m. with everyone else for "the morning run." These runs happened five days a week and were intended to build character. Clients ran in the wash (the bottom of a dry riverbed in the desert) for I don't know how many miles. It felt like ten, but I'm sure it was only one or two. By this time, I was kicking, vomiting, shivering, and sweating, my bones felt like they were splitting open, and my skin was crawling. But I was expected to run—and not just run but finish the run without quitting. It didn't matter what limitations people had, physically, emotionally, or otherwise; the idea was that if you quit on the run, then you were quitting on life. When someone looked as though they wanted to quit, others gathered around to encourage them to finish. Ironically, as much as I hated those runs, I never quit on one, probably more out of spite than for any other reason. Though I hated to admit it, the runs created movement beyond the physicality of completing them. The pressure to finish was so intense that those who didn't wound up filled with so much guilt that they often left the program the same day. After the run, we had countless activities in which we were forced to participate, keeping us busy until bedtime. There could be no idle time. Idle time and boredom for an addict were viewed as relapse triggers.

A kind gesture extended to me early on may have been the reason I stuck through that grueling first week. It came from a sixteen-year-old who understood that someone kicking heroin needed sweets. I later learned that she knew this from being raised her entire life by heroin-addicted parents. In the middle of the night, she noticed me shaking, shivering, and wide awake, so she gave me a whole bag of miniature Hershey's chocolates. I didn't even know her name at the time, but those chocolates were the best chocolates I'd ever eaten. The withdrawal rendered me sleepless for almost a month, literally. Back then there was no such thing as a medical detox for heroin addicts. It was "cold turkey" and brutal, the idea being that if you were uncomfortable enough, you would never want to feel that way again. For many, though, this was not reason enough to stop. In my experience, once the pain has passed, it is usually forgotten until it returns.

My third day there, I was put in a retreat. One might think that a retreat is a serene, spiritual, and relaxing event, but not this retreat. Retreats like the one I was in were designed to break down defenses using methods of sleep and sensory deprivation combined with emotional, physical, and mental stimulation to the point of overkill. It began with "dichotomy games." Everyone going through the retreat was brought into a room similar to a large chapel, a quite beautiful room. The participants were asked to walk clockwise in a circle while soft music was playing. The facilitator called out various life events such as rape, molestation, incarceration, and adoption, and whoever had experienced that event was to go to the center of the circle, stand there for a moment, and then step back out until the next round. It was all nonverbal except for the facilitator's voice and the music. The goal was to see how honest people would be and to learn each other's stories without the use of spoken words.

Eventually, the facilitator called for anyone who was gay to step to the center of the circle. I figured there had to be other gay people in the room. The music and atmosphere made me feel safe enough to be honest and follow the direction. But once I stepped to the center, I found myself standing completely alone in a room full of eighty strangers. I was immediately overwhelmed with feelings of utter isolation, humiliation at being different from everyone else, and vulnerability. I couldn't wait to get out of that room.

After the dichotomy games, the facilitator called off groups of ten to twelve names and sent the groups off to smaller rooms, where we spent most of the next four days. The leaders were expected to push people to have emotional and cathartic experiences in the smaller groups. I learned later, when I became a group leader, that during the retreat, the leaders met while everyone was eating to decide who was or wasn't being honest. Those persons, when group resumed, were singled out to be pushed harder to make them "cop out" to whatever lies they were telling, the parts of their life stories they were omitting, or covert misdeeds they had committed in the program. One did not want to be in that position, but in many of the retreats, my best friend Pat and I were presumed to be lying, sometimes for a reason, but more often for none, and we were pushed, hard. Both of us maintained the stance that the harder they pushed, the harder we fought, and that made it even harder on us.

Also on the premises was a Native American sweat lodge. Sweats in the Native American culture are a ceremonial cleansing and purification ritual and are sacred in their use, construction, and guidelines. The sweat lodges at Amity had been built and blessed by medicine men and were used for their intended purpose. During retreats, however, it appeared to some of us that if the staff decided someone was "dirty" with secrets and lies, that person was awakened in the middle of the night and sent there to become more forthcoming. A medicine man at the lodge stoked a fire that heated lava rocks, thereby having the ability to raise the temperature to a nearly unbearable extreme. Those sent to the sweat lodge during a retreat figured that if the staff couldn't get us to cop out to either real or perceived secrets, they were trying to sweat them out of us. This, of course, was never said out loud. For our part, Pat's and mine, we'd be damned if we were going let them win or give in, no matter how hot that sweat lodge got. Things that clients were unwilling to disclose weren't always crimes or destructive acts, such as using drugs at the program in secret or hooking up sexually with someone in the program. They could be issues people had difficulty talking about, such as certain aspects of their life stories that were shameful or intimidating. This might include defending enabling parents, defending mothers who remained silent while their husbands raped their children, or defending themselves as parents even though they were high throughout their children's lives. Pat and I were always suspected of having secrets and put on ban (meaning we weren't allowed to talk to one another until they felt our relationship was healthy and honest). Really, though, most of the time we had no secrets.

Ceremonies filled with dedications and spiritual components—mantras and prayers—from various cultures and traditions were frequent during the retreats. They were often held in the middle of the night in a pavilion and lasted up to three hours. On cold, dark winter nights, the spiritual aspect was completely lost because we were too cold, angry, or guarded at being forced to sit on hard cement benches with no sleep. During the ceremonies, the most senior staff wore black capes. Pat and I were convinced they were a cult.

In addition, some retreats included miles-long walks in the same wash where we ran every morning, but these were silent, spirit walks. During one retreat we walked to the historic and beautiful San Xavier Mission del Bac, founded in 1692 by Father Kino, a Catholic missionary. It lies on the Tohono-O'odham Indian Reservation. Father Kino died in 1711, but had built the foundation. Spanish Franciscans completed construction in 1797. It was and is the oldest, intact baroque style European structure in Arizona, still hosting mass and a school. The mission is often referred to as the White Dove of the Desert and is much worth seeing.

Despite the challenges, in retrospect, spending my first week at a retreat was the best thing that could have happened. By seeing it through, I had survived an intense and formidable aspect of the program, and even though I was kicking a mean, hard habit, I had just spent seven days of pain, regret, introspection, wonder, and learning with perfect strangers. Until that point, I had forgotten how to engage, to smile, to laugh, and to be alive and among the human race. It was one of those can't catch your breath moments. Shit, I wondered, maybe there was something to this, and still the ever-present skeptic in me wondered if they all weren't brainwashed and that I really had entered a cult. Who could know? Certainly not me, not yet.

When the retreat ended, I was assigned to the service crew, every newcomer's first job. The job duties were raking rocks and cleaning toilets. Two months later, I was promoted to the kitchen crew, which was a move up, and before long, I was a crew boss. I love to cook and feed people, and I found my niche in the kitchen. By then, I was over the withdrawal and felt healthy for the first time in many years. For women, particularly those in residential treatment programs, being healthy means gaining weight when they get clean, and then they feel like shit about it. I was no exception. I gained thirty-three pounds in two months and was bigger than I'd ever been. On more than one occasion, I was accused of eating to stuff my feelings and screamed at about it in groups, as most of the women were, but I saw my weight gain as the simple result of having access to food all day.

The atmosphere in some of those early TCs was neither kind nor safe for women. We were usually the minority. At Casa de Vida in 1975, my first TC program, I was one of only three women to the eighteen men living there. Add to this, the aggressive approaches and group dynamics of yelling, name calling, and singling people out, it was no easy road for women to walk. The differences between Casa and Amity, eleven years later, was the ratio of women to men and that there were children in residence. These changes enhanced the environment for us.

My court case was still pending. My public defender said I was still facing prison time, but he was fighting to get me sentenced to a relatively new type of probation. This new approach, termed intensive probation supervision (IPS), involved the use electronic tracking devices worn on the ankle and was initiated in response to the exploding numbers of people incarcerated both in Arizona and nationally. This increase was attributed directly to the drug epidemic and the mandatory sentencing laws attached to drug charges. As the second woman in the state to get IPS, I was mandated to complete the program. My IPS officer, an old-school, former New York City cop, let me know in no uncertain terms that if I screwed up, he wouldn't hesitate to make sure I got the twenty-eight years, no questions asked. I saw him weekly, and he checked on my progress with my counselor frequently. (Ironically, the first woman on IPS was in the program, too, and her name was also Denise; she had arrived a few months before I did. This was in 1986; and recently I made brunch at my home for Denise and Terri, another good friend from the program. Denise and I had both completed the stringent legal requirements set forth upon us and have remained friends nearly thirty years.)

One day while I was raking rocks, the program director summoned me to her office to tell me that I would be working as one of her assistants. She was known for taking on the more hardcore clients like long-time addicts and/or those few who had done time in prison. I think she figured that if I was left to my own devices, I would sabotage myself and potentially the program. I became one of her right-hand people. My duties included typing curriculum, helping with retreats, and assisting with grant/proposal requests.

In 1987, Amity applied for a grant for a jail-based program, which would be revolutionary if funded. Until then, providing rehab treatment inside jail or prison walls was unheard of in Arizona. A few in-prison drug treatment programs existed in the late 1950s and early 1960s, but they were relatively unknown and rare. Amity was awarded a small federal grant from the Department of Justice to design, implement, and run such a program in the Tucson county jail. It became a model for other states and was replicated many times throughout the country.

The ensuing year and a half was, above all, the longest I had ever not ingested, shot, or snorted any mind-altering substance. Also, however, it was a time of a deep, uncomfortable, brutally honest look into myself, my life, and how I had become who I had. It wasn't pretty, but the other side was a glimpse of who I could be, that trust could be had, and that promises and friends could be made and kept.

After I had been in the program for eighteen months, I applied for and was approved for an internship program designed for those of us who thought we might want to enter the treatment field. I was still under IPS supervision, and had nowhere to go, and nothing pressing to do, so I decided to explore this option. During the internship, I still lived in a dorm and was paid a small stipend. The first caseload handed to me consisted of eighteen people who had been deemed hardheads, like me, and who had severe and long histories of drug use, jail, and prison.

Meanwhile, a woman named Debbie I had known from prison and the streets came into the program, and I was assigned to be both her big sister and her counselor. This was a mistake. Almost immediately, I began to compromise what I had learned by showing favoritism. I made sure she had coffee and cigarettes and that all her visits were approved. This blurred the prescribed and correct lines that should be observed between counselor and client. I was working a four-days-on, three-days-off schedule and had saved enough to buy a little beater of a used car. On my days off, I started spending a lot of time with my mother, which was another mistake. I had not worked on the relationship with my mother, emotionally, psychologically, or in any way. When the subject of mothers was brought up in a group or session, I became defensive, even belligerent, or I shut down. No matter what anyone said or thought, in my eyes, my choices had been my own, and she was not at fault. I hadn't made the connection that she had enabled me for years, typical behavior for so many addicts' families. Like all enablers, my mother believed that her support for me over the years, dating back to when she would get Manny out of the house to go "dancing" while I had my friends over for heavy partying, was an expression of love, protection, and avoidance of further damage. She was oblivious to the fact that helping an active addict often kills them and their chances at recovery, so how could she have done anything wrong? She was oblivious, and so was I.

When Debbie became eligible to go out on passes from the program; we secretly met at my mom's house to hang out. We also convinced each other it was okay to drink because, after all, we were heroin addicts, not alcoholics. Our first drink was in a classy restaurant with linen tablecloths and candlelight. We split a glass of white wine. Within three weeks, we were shooting dope. At first, as it always goes, it was only occasionally, then more and more, until it was every day. Once again, I was living the parallel life, only this time more so. I was a functioning drug counselor and group facilitator, and my former, ugly, lying, scheming junkie self was back. I discovered that despite my long period off drugs, my addiction was alive and well.

CHAPTER 28
Meeting Joanne

In the spring of 1988, Pat, big sister and best friend, introduced me to her sister, Joanne, who had been arrested for embezzlement at the bank where she worked and was facing federal prison time. I was attracted to Joanne from the time I first saw her. When Pat and I went to her house, Joanne was standing over the stove stirring a big pot of something and looked as though she weighed no more than a hundred pounds. With sky-blue eyes and gorgeous, shiny, auburn hair flowing down to her waist, she looked vulnerable and childlike, nothing like the addicts I ran with. Pat and I tried to convince her that the court might let her do treatment in lieu of prison if she went there of her own accord. She wouldn't hear of it and politely, at first, declined treatment. The harder Pat and I pressed upon her the reckless, careless attitude she had, the harder she pushed back. We tried everything. She had three teenage children, and we thought surely we could "guilt" her into going for their sake. She stood her ground. A few weeks later, she violated her probation, called Pat in a panic, and asked for help, and we were able to get her mandated to the program.

She was stubborn, resistant, and skeptical about every aspect of the program and she hated being there. Somehow, through over twenty years of addiction and some degree of being streetwise so to speak, she had never been arrested, homeless, or roughed up or suffered the common consequences many addicts experienced. The four hours she spent in jail for her most recent legal predicament put the fear of something in her. She was not someone who one looked at and thought "drug addict," but then many didn't have a drug look. As is often stated, addiction does not discriminate. I spent hours espousing to her the benefits of getting clean, even though I was using on the side.

I found that when I wasn't with her, I couldn't get her out of my mind. Something about her spoke to me and drew me in immediately. I was attracted to her more every day. I knew she was straight and had never been with a woman, but it didn't matter. She was beautiful to me, inside and out. I told myself I could and would keep my feelings at bay and be content to have a platonic relationship with her. I took her under my wing and promised her that if she stayed in the program, I would be there for her. As a quasi-staff member, it was incumbent upon me to be a role model, mentor, and big sister. But of course, at this point I was in the throes of relapse. I was again hurting people with my deceit and selfishness, people who didn't have it coming.

Then it all came to an abrupt halt! The actual day I got caught went like this. As an intern, part of my job was to cater to the needs of the executive staff, doing things such as setting up their group room, preparing the coffee and snacks, and making sure the chairs were set up in a perfect circle in a spotlessly clean room. But before I could do that, I had to fix. It was early, 6:00 a.m., and I had just gotten up. I got so loaded that I left the rig and spoon on the dorm bathroom counter. When I finished setting up the group, I went back to my dorm to finish the dope I had left. The rig and spoon were gone, and I realized someone had found it. Shit! I grabbed my car keys and wallet to leave because I knew I was busted. Before I could get out of there, a client told me they wanted me in the group I had just set up. At that moment I could have left, but apparently, something about this recovery thing had stuck. For the first time in my life, I faced the music.

When I got to the group, all the staff was there, the rig and spoon were in the middle of the floor, and one empty chair awaited me. The group went for twelve hours. Then they assigned someone to watch me through the night, someone from my caseload. Talk about humbling. They kept me in the group room, got pillows and blankets, and had me sleep on the floor. I was still under the influence and drifted easily to sleep. The next morning I awoke to those all-too-familiar withdrawal symptoms. The director called me to her office, told me she had to leave for a half hour to take her husband to the doctor, and made me promise I would be there when she got back. With the most earnest humble stance I could muster and a firm handshake, I promised her I would stay put. Five minutes after she left, I tried to bolt out of the room, was straightaway tackled by four people, and kept captive until she got back. Physical restraints on people who attempted to leave these early programs were commonplace.

Upon her return, the director became so angry with me that she picked up and threw an antique rocking chair across the room. The best analogy to that moment, another instance of clarity, is the scene in *The Miracle Worker* between Anne Sullivan and Helen Keller at the water pump, when Helen Keller understands what water means, not just how to sign it. The water pump was analogous to the rocking chair. I got it! In all my years of using—drugs as well as people—no one had ever cared enough to get that angry with me. In that moment, I knew that this woman cared about my existence, and my life. In that moment I knew I was tired of and ready to stop hurting everyone in my path, even in the face of the consequences that lie ahead for using. It didn't matter. I was done with the games, the lying, and the scamming. I was done!

Against his better judgment, my IPS agent allowed me to stay in the program and accept the punishment meted out by the director. I therefore spent the better part of the next few weeks on the pew and washing pots and pans. It was spring and thus time for the spring equinox retreat (all retreats were held during the equinoxes and solstices). The retreats typically had a theme or were named; this one was called the Humor Retreat. I was in no mood for that, nor did I see the humor in anything, but it was the first time in my life that I stood accountable for my actions.

In recovery, as in life, there are "moments" of clarity. That relapse was one of those. The nature of the beast of addiction is that it is the purest form of selfishness. I didn't stay put and face the consequences of my actions for any selfish gain. It was for Joanne and Pat, and everyone else I had hurt. It was for the simple fact that in this community, I learned what real and genuine friendship and support meant. After years of treatment, therapy, and attempts to get clean, I figured that it would never happen for me, that I was a hope-to-die junkie. Being selfless was foreign to me but necessary to my eventual success. That whole notion espoused in the cliché "you can't keep it unless you give it away" really holds true. However, coming to this noble and unselfish decision was neither dignified nor without drama.

In spite of myself, my cynicism, my hopelessness, my paranoia of the cult-like feeling there, I had changed. I worked through the relapse, and a year later became an intern again and eventually became a counselor. Joanne also stayed put, too, and became an intern counselor. Over time her feelings for me grew and were reciprocated. During her first few months in the program, she ended a relationship with a man she had been with for over ten years. With its foundation being drugs, the relationship had been dysfunctional and abusive, on both their parts, but mostly his. When she chose to get clean, he didn't and the relationship ended.

We were inseparable and in love. Forming "treatment" relationships is frowned upon in residential programs, and we had to fight hard for ours. In the beginning, as those around us noticed how close we were, many groups "confronted" our inappropriate friendship, which for a long time was only a friendship. In time, however, it became clear to everyone that we were going to be together, and we couldn't have asked for more support. The background song to our first kiss was Melissa Etheridge's "Watching You," and every kiss was pure magic from that moment on. She said that making love to me felt natural to her, although we waited months before finally consummating us. The anticipation, the flirting, and the waiting made it more perfect than it might have been, if that's possible. The first time we made love was soft, pure, gentle, and so deeply intimate, for by then we had waited nearly a year. It was as if both our lives we had waited, longed for, and finally reached a place we had never been, and never would leave.

Between us, we were making a few hundred dollars a month. Joanne still had a home that her youngest daughter, Danielle, owned. Danielle had been hit by a service vehicle at age eleven and was sixteen when Joanne went into the program. Danielle had received a settlement from the accident and Joanne had helped Danielle buy the house. We moved off the facility and in with Danielle and Joanne's son, Paul, who was eighteen. She had another daughter, Kim, who was nineteen and had since moved out. As with any mother who has a history of addiction, Joanne had done significant and hard work throughout her time in treatment and for years to follow. For the most part, however, the kids accepted and supported her choice to be in a gay relationship with me. To my surprise, this love, this woman, this life took me somewhere I'd never been, a place of perfection and bliss, even with the struggles Joanne faced with the kids. I was happy to be a part of that process with her and for her. I had always believed that Diana was the soul mate of my life and that I would never love that way again, but what she and I had didn't come close to how I felt with Joanne. I felt safe, whole, and head over heels in love and couldn't believe my good fortune in finding love, again, but this one soared above all the others prior. My heart had never been so full.

PART FOUR

BACK TO PRISON

CHAPTER 29
Redemption

In 1991, Amity got a contract to start a drug program in San Diego inside the walls of the Donovan State Prison. I was offered the opportunity with a substantial raise in pay to commute back and forth between California and Arizona to help start it. For over a year, I traveled regularly between Tucson and San Diego. Joanne was still working at the Tucson facility, but often went to San Diego with me. It was such a refreshingly different atmosphere, green, lush, no 100 degree summers, and an ocean. On one such trip, we drove along the 163, a short freeway stretch that goes through the middle of Balboa Park. The day we drove that route was, I believe, the day we decided to move to San Diego; it was just too perfect and beautiful not to. Joanne was transferred and hired as assistant to the director.

Prisons are classified on levels from one to five according to the type of crimes and histories of the inmates housed there, with a level five prison having the most violent, hardened, and resistant criminals. As Donovan was a level three prison, the men there were pretty tough and definitely hardcore. Amity at Donovan was one of the first two in-prison drug programs in the state, with 200 men participating. The other was an eighty-bed program called Forever Free, inside the California Institution for Women in Norco, California, which had started within months of Amity. Within ten years, research proved that both programs reduced recidivism to unprecedented lows.

The attitude among the inmates on the yard at Donovan about treatment, however, was that anyone who went into a drug program had to be a snitch. Because the program was voluntary, we had to convince them that the program was of some benefit to them. We had our stories. We walked the yard and tried to target the shot-callers because we knew that if we could get them to buy in, they would get others to do the same. Our strategy worked. We soon filled every treatment slot. At first, working in this environment was an unexpected, and certainly unwanted, journey backward, backward to the interactions I had had with men up to that point in my life, experiences that left me on guard and nervous about going to work. But I persevered, and oh, what a road lie ahead.

There were only two female counselors and Elaine, the program director, who worked inside the prison. All three of us had histories of abuse by men and unresolved anger, pain, and hurt. Add to this, the issues that the men in the program had and we were all on what at times felt like a harrowing ride. Most women who work in an all-male environment such as a prison or drug treatment program become targets for the men's issues, which is as it should be in terms of the client/counselor interaction. When boundaries were set and respected, our role was to represent every woman who had ever hurt, betrayed, or left them. In clinical terms, transference, displacement, and projection are common in the realm of counselor/client interactions. The expectation is that counselors are professional, whole and strong enough to withstand being targets and eventually to allow clients to learn that one woman does not define all women, and vice versa in women's programs, that there are healthy relationships, etc. I spent much of the first two years feeling afraid, angry, and upset. Logically, I knew these were my issues, but emotionally—especially when one of the men in the program articulated, in graphic detail, how he had raped someone—it almost broke me. Ironically, however, this was the path by which I was able to forgive men, and many of these convicts ended up learning the role of big brothers or protectors rather than abusers.

We had a daily trek each morning past hundreds of men, most who were not in the program, to get to our module. We were subject to lascivious looks and catcalls from the men who worked out on the weight pile. Over time, if one of the men in the program witnessed these crude gestures, the guys on the weight pile got "checked" by the guys in the program. As I listened, learned, and grew more comfortable, I learned to separate the person from the behavior and to understand that even the most heinous crimes were, more often than not, committed as a response to the crimes that had been committed against these perpetrators when they were children. I learned that men and women respond to pain differently and that men suffer injustice at the hands of cultural conditioning that compels them to be strong, to fight, and to mask their feelings. When the men at Donovan felt safe enough to express themselves, we discovered that they were little boys inside muscle-bound, tattooed bodies, just little boys who had been deeply hurt. But more importantly, they were men who could change, starting by allowing themselves to feel and cry, even to sob. For any counselor fortunate enough to witness and be a part of that process, it is deeply touching.

Life in San Diego was just good. Finally, and to my utter amazement and gratitude, my life had the stability, sense of purpose, and love I had always craved but never knew how to grab hold of. It turns out my craving for these things had to be greater than my craving for drugs. For many, perhaps most, this never happens. I guess I was just lucky.

In 1993, Joanne and I were asked to open and live as on-site managers at a residential aftercare program for the men coming out of the in-prison program. Our boss thought that a feminine influence would help. Newly built, the facility was a forty-bed, ranch-style place on green and flourishing acres of land, with a creek running through a portion of the property in Vista, about thirty miles north of San Diego. The wealthy owner had originally built it as a Twelve Step recovery program site for affluent drug addicts and alcoholics. She had never been able to get it off the ground, however, and it had been vacant for quite some time. The first thirteen men arrived, and Joanne and I moved into a room just like theirs, where we lived for eight months. The men, or "fellas" as I affectionately called them, grew very fond and protective of us and dependent on our feedback and guidance. Once the program reached capacity, not all of the clients were as accepting or unbiased at the notion of living with two lesbians. There were those who acted out, broke rules, and cursed out everyone in the place. But overall, Joanne and I were treated with the utmost respect, and it was one of the most moving experiences in our twenty-four years together.

By 1998, and after twelve years with Amity, I was capped as far as career and salary. A friend and colleague told me about another agency, Mental Health Systems, Inc. (MHS), which according to her, was a great company where I could advance my career. The first time I applied there, I didn't get hired, so I returned to school and finished my Bachelor of Arts at National University. I had had enough credits for a BA twenty years earlier but I was so far gone at the time that I didn't finish the process. California accepted most of my credits, but I had to take nine classes to meet California residency requirements. Universities such as these for working adults offer fast-paced, one-class-a-month, crash courses. Each month yielded three credits, and each month I had to write at least two term papers and pass weekly, midterm, and final exams. The months flew by as I continued to work full time and had no life outside work and school, but I knew the sacrifice would pay off.

I graduated summa cum laude. The very month I graduated, MHS called me with a job offer. The starting salary was the same as what it had taken me twelve years to earn at my current employer and within a year at MHS, my degree paid for itself. Education truly lends itself to opportunity and freedom.

The old expression "good things happen in threes" proved true when, in addition to graduating and getting a new job, Joanne and I had a commitment ceremony. It was our tenth year together. Even though at the time our union was not regarded, recognized, or accepted as a wedding, it was that and more. We were among a community that saw it as a wedding and made it perhaps more wondrous an occasion that it might have been if we had been part of the norm. Joanne was stunningly beautiful that day, and I couldn't imagine loving her more, loving us more, and loving our life together. The men in the program catered all the food, did flower arrangements, and built a beautiful wooden arbor under which we vowed our eternal love in front of an amazingly diverse community—a human rainbow certainly—on that unforgettable perfect spring day in May. We had about a hundred guests, most of them straight. Alongside former Compton gang members, Aryan nation, and Mexican mafia were gays and lesbians, children, and elderly people. Joanne and I each had a best man and maid of honor. Her son, Paul, gave her to me, and my mother gave me to her. Throughout the years, my mother and I had worked hard on repairing our complex and addiction-worn relationship, and her giving me away to Joanne at this ceremony represented the culmination of our efforts. Joanne's three children had by then come to respect and love the relationship between their mother and me and viewed me as their "other mother." The ceremony was and remains to this day a gift and a memory that lingers so sweetly, a time in our life as a couple that showed the ability of people to overcome prejudice, celebrate love, and practice tolerance and acceptance. It brought out the best in us and in everyone present, this heartwarming display of what community can accomplish.

The day after the commitment ceremony was graduation commencement at the San Diego Convention Center downtown. The next day I began my new job—three major life-changing events in three days! MHS and my new job were quite the contrast from Amity. It was a completely new arena, a company with over five hundred employees and nearly a hundred programs throughout California. My first position was to help start a new contract that MHS had just been awarded called SARMS (Substance Abuse Recovery Management System), which was a collaborative effort between MHS, Child Protective Services, and San Diego Family Court. My boss and I literally started with two beach chairs in an empty office. From that tiny empty office came a program with four regional sites, over eight hundred parents and their dependent children, and fifty case managers. Parents whose children had been removed because of abuse or neglect were mandated to our office for assessment and placement into appropriate drug and alcohol treatment. Almost without exception, the children had been removed from the homes because of their parents' drug or alcohol use. The presiding Juvenile Court judge, Honorable Judge James R. Milliken, was instrumental in securing funding for the program. Throughout his years on the bench, he witnessed the long-term damage to children in foster care, who were then spending an average of five years in foster homes before their cases were resolved. Many of the children had been in multiple placements. Judge Milliken concluded, rightly so, that what was happening to the children was detrimental to their emotional development, well-being, and ability to grow, love, learn, and evolve. He was passionate and adamant that change was needed. He was finally able to get San Diego County to issue a request for proposals, and MHS got the contract. His specific, direct intent, as well as the contractual requirements, was to shorten children's time in foster care and whenever or however possible to reunify the children with their parent(s) within eighteen months versus the previous five-year process. The program succeeded not only in reducing the average time in foster care to half what it had been, but also in reunifying a great number of parents with their children, and it saved the county millions of dollars.

213

I got to know the judge pretty well, and as far as I was concerned, he was light-years ahead of his peers. He was down to earth, funny, genuine, and so very curious in cases where he had no experience. In one such instance, a woman who was on methadone maintenance appeared before him, and technically, this would have disqualified her for the program. Before ruling on her case, however, he called my boss to get his feedback and requested that someone from SARMS go with him to the methadone clinic. He wanted to be fully informed before ruling. I was asked to go and I met him for breakfast, at his insistence, before going to the clinic. Upon hearing that I had once been a heroin addict and knew a little bit about methadone, he wanted to know everything! Such humility for someone in his position, and another one of his many qualities that others should emulate. He ruled that the mother in question was appropriate for the program, and she completed it, got off methadone, and was reunified with her two young children.

CHAPTER 30
New Starts

A year and a half later, MHS was awarded a new contract to design and implement a 300-bed drug program in a women's prison in Norco, California (the horse capital of the US). I was offered the job of program manager, which came with another substantial pay raise. Joanne and I relocated to a small, conservative town called Lake Elsinore. When the dust settled—and in the desert town of Lake Elsinore, this applied literally and figuratively—I began to realize the magnitude of the job and panicked several times over the next few weeks. I had never worked on anything this big and had never managed anything other than a long-standing drug habit. The program was to be housed in a double-wide trailer that was being built and designed specifically to provide treatment. It was August, but the trailer wasn't finished yet, so we started in the prison gym. It wasn't until December that the trailer construction was completed.

The women we worked with were mandated to the program. On the first day, the first 150 of those who had been classified to start treatment reported to the gym, and they were pissed off, disrespectful, and just plain ugly about being forced to participate. Before they were required to report to us, they had had pay numbers, but now they had lost their wage of twenty or thirty cents an hour. This may not sound like much, but it's a good wage in prison. The lessons I had learned working in the men's prison at Donovan quickly came to bear. I knew that we had to do three things to get them to buy in: first, we had to target the shot callers; second, we had to use our experience, strength, and hope in an effort to lead them gently rather than direct them (an assertion borrowed from Alcoholics Anonymous); and third, we had to build community in a place that was the antithesis of that. Being in the gym presented its own challenges. In addition to having no air conditioning or fans during August temperatures of 100 degrees and over, the gym's poor acoustics resulted in all conversation being echoed. Swarms of bees circled around our breakout groups, which were held every morning and afternoon inside and outside the gym.

Nevertheless, I delved into my role quickly and was able to sell to the staff the notion of "community building" as an element critical to our success. Honestly, the team we found and hired was amazing and courageous just to show up every day under such adverse conditions, so much resistance from the women, and flak from the prison staff, who made it clear they were not in favor of drug programs. The women were convicts first and foremost, and they put us through constant tests. They cursed us out, disrespected us, ran games on us, and generally gave us hell. We tasked them with naming the program and writing a philosophy (common in many programs). They did both, coming up with New Starts as a name and stating their beliefs about how it should be run. Over time, some of them began to wonder if perhaps what we were selling might be worth buying—a different life, one without the misery and heartbreak that comes with drug and alcohol use, and a tiny glimmer of hope that one can get out of prison and never go back. Eighty percent of the women were mothers who had abandoned, lost, or given up their children and deemed unfit by most of society because they put drugs and alcohol before their children.

The stigma attached to female addicts is so very different from that for males, for a few reasons. Areas of concern exclusive to women such as motherhood—particularly failure at it among female addicts—prostitution, and abortion are highly charged emotional issues, causing female addicts to have far more shame and guilt than their male counterparts. Society is quick to single them out, judge, and persecute them rather than dig deeper and understand that an addict is an addict is an addict, and when people are addicted, their actions are involuntary. Their ability to choose is gone. Although they may commit despicable acts to feed their addiction, when one graduates from using to being addicted, his or her actions become a necessity versus a choice. This fact is lost on those outside the realm of drug and alcohol treatment, although in recent years there has been more education about addiction. One only need look as far as television, for example, *Intervention*, *Relapse*, *Dr. Drew Pinsky's Celebrity Rehab*, *The Biggest Loser*, and hundreds of other documentaries and popular movies, to see that far more awareness and information are being circulated and entering the mainstream. Even so, female addicts still face distorted and ill-conceived perceptions about their morality and decency. In my experience, I have witnessed no guilt worse than that of a mother who has lost, abandoned, or hurt her children. Even when she begins to understand that while she was addicted she was unable to make any other choices, the guilt consumes her. Thus, the work women must do to overcome the guilt and shame, imposed both upon them and within them, is so much more an arduous journey than it is for men.

Working in prisons, both men's and women's, was profoundly rewarding. Filled with heartbreak and miracles, it reached into vast realms of human emotion. My team and I worked in a place where we had to foster growth, warmth, and hope in an unwelcoming, harsh, ugly environment. We were privy to women's secrets, heartbreaking ones such as how male guards had sneaked into their cells at night and raped them or the constant harassment and comments they were subjected to from both male and female guards. These women had no voice, no power, and no support. We were witness to women who started doing prison time on the wrong foot by, for instance, saying yes to the wrong convict and thus becoming someone else's "property," able to be bought, sold, or traded for a pack of smokes. We were witness to the stories of women from all walks of life who had been beaten, broken, exploited, raped, and oppressed in places where they painfully learned that to survive they must either oppress or be oppressed because there was no in between. We were witness to the "black market" that came to be when smoking was banned in the California prisons, and tobacco was worth more than any drug on the yard. This policy created yet another context for extortion, blackmail, and violence. One woman in the program had convinced a younger, weaker woman to get her mother to smuggle tobacco into the prison during visitation. When the mother got scared and decided to stop, the one who had been getting and selling the tobacco had friends on the outside threaten the mother and the rest of the family unless she continued to bring it in. The mother called the prison authorities, prompting an investigation. Shortly after this, her daughter was attacked in her sleep with a heavy metal lock inside a sock, placing the girl in a hospital for over a month. Warden Gordon, who couldn't have been more supportive of the program, the captain, and I isolated the perpetrator and then shipped her to a higher custody level prison in Northern California the following week. But this wasn't the first, nor would it be the last, episode of violence brought on by outlawing tobacco.

The first year working with the New Starts program brought back all my ugliest prison memories, haunting images of things I didn't want to remember. The senseless beatings, the hole, the racism, the rampant oppression and extortion by both guards and inmates alike, the injustice of the disparity in sentencing, the weak inmates versus the strong convicts all flooded back like a turbulent, raging wave out of a dark sea, so much more vividly in the women's prison than in the men's prison. Once again I was grappling with that troubling dynamic of the oppressed oppressing each other, now from the perspective of working in a prison. Knowing I had been one of the oppressors during my five years inside, I always told myself I had to do it to survive. But on a gut level, I knew there had come a point when that reason no longer applied, that I had crossed over to a place of just being a cruel, heartless person joining the ranks of those to be feared and liking how that felt. Perhaps this work was a means to an end, to balance the karmic debt I figured I owed the universe for all the pain I had inflicted on family, friends, and innocent victims. The fearless team I was so fortunate to have working with me accomplished nothing short of a miracle by building community within a prison, a place where the opposite of kinship generally thrives. No easy task, to be sure.

By Thanksgiving, only three months since the program's inception, we received permission from the Warden to bring in Thanksgiving dinner with all the trimmings. All the staff spent a week prior to the event preparing various dishes, and we served the women dinner following an incredibly moving ceremony. By then, I had spent years working with convicts, criminals, and addicts with the intent of helping them out of their misery and pain, in the company of others who had already found their way. On Thanksgiving Day, I wrote and read what follows to the New Starts community.

I have known:

A woman who wrote in the autobiography she was asked to do on her treatment plan: 'My nightmare as a child began the day I was born. My mother was addicted to heroin.'

A daughter who begged her mother to come out of a 'nod' to just talk to her.

A mother 'nodded-out' for twenty-five years who never considered the option of stopping. Her grown son didn't know her without heroin.

A man who has served twenty-five years for a murder in a drug deal gone bad. He has more character and goodness than most people I know.

A fifty-eight-year-old woman who remembers a rage deep enough for her to want to kill her stepfather at age seventeen. She stopped because of the tears in her baby brother's eyes.

A young man serving life for putting a gun to his crack dealer's head. The crack dealer who pressed charges owns an apartment complex where he sells crack to women and children.

A woman robbed, attacked, and raped by three ski-masked men. Twenty-five years later, she can't be in a house alone at night. Nights changed forever.

A child with no childhood, born addicted to heroin—yet still innocent and naïve—and later so filled with pain, and finally taken out by five bullets in his chest.

A bright, young woman who mutilates herself with sharp objects to erase another pain that feels worse to her.

A man whose only dream was to have a television in his cell.

A woman out of prison twenty-one years, haunted still by the memories of the times she 'sold out' morally to 'survive.'

Men and women that lust desperately to ingest something into their noses, mouths, veins, eventually their souls—to escape the pain of their existence.

I have known men and women who lived, fell to the bottom stayed there, or came up. It's about coming up, simple but so difficult.

Denise Sassoon

We all had stories that brought us to that day, that moment. They were stories of pain, trauma, betrayal, loss, and grief, as well as bliss, laughter, and love. The key in overcoming the pain of those stories was to integrate, cherish, and share them. In doing so, we had found, even if just for a brief space in time, peace of mind, gratitude, and humility in knowing that bittersweet fact that somewhere someone was worse off. Someone was mourning a loss that words couldn't express. Somewhere a man, woman, or child was dying of AIDS, or a grandmother spent Thanksgiving alone because her children's lives were too busy. Somewhere a child cowered in a corner, afraid of the beating to come. Somewhere a mother cowered in a shelter, her eyes blackened after the beating, and somewhere unkind strangers avoided the hollow empty eyes of the homeless man who asked for spare change. I was so filled with gratitude that Thanksgiving for all that I had learned and witnessed, and that I could share it. I had the privilege of dreaming for people who couldn't yet dream for themselves.

After the ceremony, we danced to "Heaven Must Have Sent You" by Bonnie Pointer, one of my all-time favorite songs, in that same gym, where they had poured out their hearts, tears, and stories to us and to one another. It was a testament to the notion that such deep extremes of pain could lead to far greater extremes of bliss and joy.

CHAPTER 31
Providence Place and More

With Joanne busy running the administrative offices that supported several of the MHS programs, work was phenomenal for both of us. We loved our jobs, the company, and going to work every day. We were both learning and growing professionally, and our hard work was rewarding and rewarded. Unfortunately, however, the town we had moved to was not. We discovered that it was extremely conservative and racist and anyone who was different—in other words, gay people and people of color—stood the risk of suffering hate crimes. It sucked because we had bought a house for the first time, a beautiful two-story, three-bedroom house on a huge corner lot with a pool. At work, we met another gay couple who needed a place to stay, and we had more than enough room for them to move in with us. It wasn't long before we started getting harassed. Our house was egged and vandalized, and all four of us felt strongly that we were at risk or worse. They had succeeded, run us out of their little perfect town!

I called the corporate office to see if there were any positions back in San Diego and as luck would have it, they were looking for someone to manage a mothers and children's residential drug program. Joanne's position was flexible enough that she could just move her office to the San Diego branch. Our roommates moved, and we sold the house and moved back to San Diego. The program awaiting me there, called Providence Place, was an eighty-bed residential program for women coming out of prison. If their children met the criteria, they were allowed to reside at the program with their mothers and could stay up to eighteen months. But the place was a disaster when I arrived on the scene. There had been no manager for four months. The staff had barely held it together. They were burnt out and at each other's throats. Located in one of the worst areas of San Diego, a gang-ridden neighborhood in the southeast section of the city, the program was on the fourth floor of a five-story, sixty-year-old, run-down hospital. There was no playground for the kids, with the exception of a small park across the street filled with homeless people, drug addicts, used syringes and condoms, paraphernalia, and broken liquor bottles. The challenge was to end the chaos and find a balance between nurturing and accountability.

My first day there, I encountered the inmates "running the asylum," so to speak, cursing out the staff and refusing to work or go to group. To make a point, I threw a woman out who was especially disruptive and threatening. This wasn't my style and a tactic I used sparingly, but the staff needed to see they were going to have support, and the clients needed to see that business as usual was over. It worked, and within a year, Providence Place—just like New Starts—had become a community. Of all the jobs I held, this was the most personally moving, even more so than in the prisons. It was the first time I worked with children. The Department of Corrections funded it, and the contract required that children in residence had to be between ages newborn and twelve years. Each mother was allowed two children. More often than not, however, a mother had more than two children, and she had to choose which two would join her in the program. A difficult and horrible choice to have to make, I thought, but it was better than no access to treatment.

The greatest regret of my own life is that I did not have children, and this has left a gaping emptiness that has stayed with me, some years worse than others, but still a regret. My life's work and the love I shared with Joanne helped fill the void, and yet widened it too at times. Thus, at Providence, when a newborn baby came into the world, into the program, I was especially ecstatic. The clients and staff frequently found me with one and sometimes two babies in my office while I worked at my desk. The toddlers often ran to hug me upon my arrival to work in the morning; their little legs couldn't run fast enough to get to me, smiling all the way down the hall.

During my seven-year tenure there, I found myself in complete harmony with the staff, the clients, and the kids. It was a combination of the right time, the right team, and even the right place. As terrible as the physical environment was, it worked because we made it work.

Christmas and Thanksgiving were especially moving. Every year the staff were allowed to pick either Christmas or Thanksgiving to work, and so many of them sacrificed time with their own families to come to work, serve the clients, their families, and children. In the lives of most addicts, holidays become meaningless and are a nuisance because they make it harder to take care of the business of getting well. Some of the children had never experienced a real Christmas, and women who had been in and out of prison for decades had few or no memories of holidays. This made the ceremonies and taking time out to express gratitude for the gift of being out of prison, off drugs, and alive so essential, just as essential as any curriculum or relapse prevention class.

The ceremonies weren't so much religious as they were spiritual, and there are noteworthy differences. Throughout my career, I have seen the unethical, illegal emphasis on religion in state-funded programs and prisons, particularly traditional Christianity. The women in the program told us of a correctional officer who made it widely known that the best way to get him to process release paperwork in a timely fashion was to attend his Bible class study. Those who did not attend found themselves last on his list of priorities. He couldn't explicitly require this, but it was just known and understood. There remain strong implications in most prisons and programs that "getting God" or "getting religion" is the way to get ahead, get a parole date, or get "positive" reviews. These practices are morally and legally objectionable. In an article about that line between spirituality and religion, Rabbi Rami Shapiro wrote:

> Religion is often about who's in and who's out, creating a world-view steeped in "us against them." Spirituality rejects this dualism and speaks of them and us. Religion is often about loyalty to institutions, clergy and rules while Spirituality is about loyalty to justice and compassion." ('Spirituality and Health," *Home Magazine*, May/June, 2012)

Rabbi Shapiro thought the two need not be at odds, but so often they are. There were Muslims, Catholics, Native Americans, atheists, and everyone in between, both in the program and in the prison. Our charge was to find and maintain that delicate spiritual balance that left no one excluded, which is as it should be anywhere not just in prison.

Our efforts in the mothers and children's program were very successful. Aside from the formal treatment, we organized monthly beach trips, camping trips, and other excursions. One such excursion was to the Museum of Tolerance in Los Angeles. Every few months we took ten or fifteen of the clients to the museum and spent the following day in a workshop with discussion and curriculum on racism and bigotry. We wanted the women to think bigger, to understand how pervasive these intolerances have been in history and, closer to home, and how prison reinforces these ills. We wanted them to buy out, so to speak, of bigotry and racism instead of buying in, as so many of them had by virtue of spending so many years on the streets, in gangs, and in prison; it's just part of the culture in those environments. Years later, the staff and the women recounted this particular experience as life changing.

We had the privilege of guiding and then watching women change and make amends to their children. Thus, the children were healing too. The focus of everything was to create a safe home for the children who had been exposed to, experienced, and done things no child should ever have to see or do. In my view, nothing is better than the work of making the world safer and better for children, and these children affected by the addiction of their parent were especially hurt, wounded, vulnerable, and damaged. Their stories were tragic and incomprehensible, even though logically one may understand that addiction is a chronic, lifelong, potentially fatal disease over which addicts have no control while actively practicing their compulsion. The unintentional and yet devastating consequences for the children are beyond heartbreaking, beyond words, beyond what those unfamiliar with this invisible segment of the larger community can fathom. Women and kids who lived five minutes from the beach their whole lives had never seen the ocean (hence the therapeutic value of three-day camping trips to San Elijo). Women who sold out or traded their children to pimps, ex-cons, and drug dealers for a hit off a crack pipe or a fix of heroin had left their kids in harm's way to get raped, beaten, starved, and neglected. They professed love for their children, which was met with disdain by societal standards and their families. But we believed them. We had to, just to last, to listen and learn, to make sense of the senseless to ourselves to process the details of stories and lives no one wants to hear or know about. We knew deep down, they meant those words, but to reconcile what the children had gone through with parents they did not choose or deserve wasn't always easy, even for us professionals in this field, and was the impetus for countless sleepless nights.

I stood by Joanne's side through years of therapy and work she so courageously did to make right the pain she had brought upon her children, who by then I loved as my own. They have struggled with their own demons through the years, and Joanne's deepest desire was to right her wrongs. I thought her so brave to sit in family groups while they laid into her, lashed out at her, and felt safe enough to tell her how they felt. In my heart of hearts, knowing I may be biased, I believe she did as much as any mother could. Her oldest son thrives; he is a paramedic, married, and lives in Alaska. Her youngest, a daughter, is mother to two beautiful children and happily married, and her middle daughter is close to a degree in business. She, and they, came out of those difficult and dark times.

One might suppose that doing this work for over twenty years would render the thousands of stories one hears redundant or commonplace. But it never ceases to amaze and startle me when I hear a new one. The details matter. The details of a young woman having both legs broken after being hit with a detached kitchen sink by a raging boyfriend in a crack- or meth-induced psychotic episode. The details of a five-year-old who was labeled hyperactive and prescribed psychotropic drugs after he bit the school's vice principal. The details in the sad eyes of an eighteen-month-old baby girl with absolutely no affect—no tears, no smiles, no emotional affect whatsoever—after never or rarely having been rocked, nurtured, or touched. The details of the woman who came in during the first trimester of her eighth pregnancy who never had custody of the previous seven babies she'd carried, all of them crack babies and in different foster or adoptive homes. It was a tremendous effort for our team to convince Child Protective Services (and even ourselves) to give her another chance. The details of another woman who spent so many years in prison being beaten that her head hung low, and she could not grasp the concept of trust for anyone, even enough to have a conversation during mealtime because she couldn't make eye contact with the person sitting across from her. The details of all those who went to treatment the first time and never looked back, as well as the ones who tried fifteen or twenty times to get clean, only to overdose and die a week after leaving treatment. The details of that one counselor who had been to prison, used drugs, and had four or five years clean under her belt when she was found trapped inside a car, burned beyond recognition, presumably at the hands of an ex-boyfriend. Her story didn't even make the local evening news—she was poor, black, a nonperson to everyone but us. The details matter! Her story mattered! In honor of her life, Pamela Kelly wrote the following poem for Black History Month one year:

> What's my nationality?
> What difference does it make?
> Will it make you love or hate me?
> Or treat me second rater?
> Ask me how my heart is,
> It beats the same as yours
> Ask me of my convictions
> With them I open doors
> Ask about my parents,
> I have two, same as you.
> They come from a race called human
> And yours did too.

I was now trained, and even more, I wanted to pay attention to the details after years of blocking them out.

CHAPTER 32
Hope

I spent over twenty years nodded out behind the mask of heroin, five of them in prison. I don't regret those years. They are integral threads in the tapestry of my being. What I do regret is how many people were hurt, the many who crossed my path and were victims of my crimes, my addiction, my misery, and my disdain for life.

Twenty-seven years ago I was lucky enough to find a place, a safe place, where I could become conscious rather than unconscious and begin practicing good deeds rather than destructive ones. I was lucky enough to find boundless love with a woman who was decent, precious, and beautiful. The years are now full with all the exquisite range of human emotions I spent so many years trying to avoid or pretend didn't exist.

Before that, my problem was that I had not been relentless in trying to figure out my contempt for life and love for drugs. When I got to the program in 1986, I was thirty-three years old and a bitter, jaded, cynical dope fiend facing twenty-eight years back in prison for felony thefts. I had crossed every line I said I wouldn't, and even drew new ones of self-degradation. The result was that I was in pain, and caused pain to others. I was in the program to beat my felony cases, kick my habit, and get healthy enough to start another run. Period. However, I found myself in a place where I had to take a brutal, honest look at my life and begin accepting responsibility for it. I was cynical and angry. I don't think I suffered some great injustice. I used to think I had, but have learned that all of my experiences make me who I am. I used to blame everyone else for my lot in life, and thought the world owed me because I sometimes got dealt a shitty hand growing up. When I learned that my responses to the

227

shitty hand I was dealt, the anger, resentment, and cynicism, were choices, I changed. I learned that all-too-important lesson: we may not have choices about what happens to us, but we do have choices about how to respond. I worked with those whom I saw myself in and for whom I saw possibility. On some level, I figured I had a moral debt to the universe to be paid by working to prevent people from doing harm to themselves and others, particularly their children. I can only hope that, in part, that debt was paid.

I never thought that offenders are victims, except of their own ignorance and the ignorance of others. I don't think they should be coddled either. I know they can be reached. I have worked with people related to top correction officials, the Qualcomm family, major-league football and baseball players, actors, politicians, as well as those who are invisible on the back stairs of society, where poverty, crime, drugs, and violence have been their only point of reference for living. More than anything, they have been regarded and labeled as useless, hopeless, nonpersons to be ignored, written off, and thrown away. They need teaching about society, about decency, about themselves. For some, this learning begins with basic hygiene. They need lots of tiny pushes from people who believe in their potential and value as human beings.

For over twenty years, I have worked with hundreds of men and women who marked time behind prison walls, day by day, hour by hour, and minute by minute. I have listened to them struggling to make their lives mean something. I listened to their tears, their pain, their regrets, and their guilt. And later, joyfully, I have heard their eventual recovery and movement into laughter, amends, and consciousness. I am ever humbled by this work that encompasses the paradox of miracles arising out of misery.

The feat of realizing one's potential is a journey that does not end when a man or woman goes to a treatment program or completes the aftercare program. It goes on. Helen Keller said: "Life is either a daring adventure or nothing. To keep our faces toward change and behave like free spirits in the presence of fate is strength undefeatable."

The men and women still incarcerated by prison, drugs, or the streets must learn and become adventurous and daring enough to change. They mustn't forget that with freedom comes personal and moral responsibility. The families who so graciously support them must remain hopeful, yet non-enabling. Everyone must understand how powerful, difficult, and gut wrenching the work of changing a life can be and must remain in awe of this, for it is no less than awesome. Those who do change their lives must continue to grow in realism, courage, wisdom, strength, and persistence in finding the good in themselves. I have always loved this quote: "The sky starts at your feet; think how brave you are to walk around."

I pay tribute to the committed and courageous counselors, teachers, childcare professionals, law enforcement, therapists, nurses, social workers, and anyone in a "helping" profession. They demonstrate that change is necessary and possible. Some have walked that hard road from addiction, degradation, and shame toward lives of dignity and honor. Some haven't, but were touched by that inestimable commodity called empathy. These are men and women with voices, and passionate about giving other men and women a voice. They are heroes to me and to be commended on hard work, relentless pursuit for knowledge, and just hanging in there no matter how hard it gets.

My life is rich with joy, sorrow, grief, pain, laughter, travel, friends, and miracles, each year better than the one before it.

I pay tribute to the men in my life, both those who hit, hurt, and raped me and those who were gentle, loving, and protective of me, and of Joanne. The men who sat in those rooms with me in groups and allowed themselves to become vulnerable, allowed themselves to be the hurt little boys that were inside their muscle-bound exteriors, and in so doing, healed their own deep wounds. I pay tribute to their selfless gestures toward me that made it safe, and that safety helped me forgive.

I pay tribute to the women I've had the honor of meeting, learning from, growing with, and joining arms with toward a shared dream of finding the way out of the dark. We were raised to compete with each other, to see each other as enemies. We were raised to see ourselves as inferior. I watched the women in my life struggle, cry, laugh, and work diligently to overcome obstacles and become better than they ever thought they could be. I am they, they are me, and we are not "less than." No one can take our identity or spirit from us. As Eleanor Roosevelt said, "No one can make you feel inferior without your consent." If we stay true to this belief and to ourselves, there is no limit to what we can achieve.

Denise Sassoon

I pay tribute to my brothers, Jonathan and Nate, and my sweet baby sister, Jeanette. I pay tribute to all my extended family. Through far too many years of witnessing my suicide mission, they stood behind me. I was not the big sister I should have been, and I continue my amends. They have all come into their own, with children and grandchildren. Jonathan and Nate are both husbands, fathers, and gentle men who did their utmost to counter the men in their lives who were the antithesis of gentle men. Jeanette, so brave and strong, was my mother's caretaker. She and my mother lived together for most of forty years, and Jeanette sacrificed over eight years of her life to walk with my mother through time, age, pain, and finally her passing. She then went on to pursue her dream of long-haul truck driving, and my greatest wish for her is that she live her life and find the happiness she has coming for the selfless generosity of love she showered upon our sweet dear mother.

I pay tribute to my mother whom, as is often the way, I didn't fully understand or appreciate until my thirties. She was a woman of such silent strength, a woman who took life in such soft stride even though life was anything but soft for her, but in fact hard and challenging. She remains, objectively, the most patient, unassuming, tolerant, cherished, and loving person I have ever met or will ever meet. Of this, I am sure. Those who knew her would say the same. Through her last couple of years, she recovered from a broken hip, pneumonia, and the myriad ailments that come at eighty-five years old. Osteoporosis and arthritis had crippled her. Despite all these, she kept an optimism and love for life that I've rarely witnessed, and hope that I have emulated those qualities through my own life. We lost her just a short time ago, and while I sat with her as she drew her final breath, there was a peace, a beauty in that moment, as if she was tired, ready. Perhaps in time, I'll be ready too, but not now. Not yet, not so soon between that loss and the loss of my wife, my partner, my all.

I pay tribute to Joanne, her life, her work, her nurturing ways, her sweet blue eyes, and flowing auburn hair, like gold. During our twenty-five years of bliss and beauty, love and support, we experienced weddings, births, deaths, cancer, career, everything! Not one day, not one minute passed that I wasn't filled with awe, excitement, and butterflies in my stomach when I knew I would see her, even just after the twenty minutes it took to run to the grocery store.

Grief, since her passing in October 2012 and my mother's in September 2013, is foreign to me. I've survived prison, rape, addiction, pain, deep unparalleled empathy and pain for the men and women throughout my career, but none of these compares to grief. I dreamed of walking into a prison someday and walking back out of my own accord. I dreamed of one day writing a book. I've had dreams and realized those dreams. I've had love and lovers, many, and each occupies a special sacred piece of my heart. When Joanne passed away, I had horrible and disturbing images of me, past 60 years old with none of my own teeth (technically I do own them, just not the originals), wrinkled, with time and life, and lacking the energy that my twenty-year-old soul craves. I imagined I would live, be, and die alone, homeless on the streets. Grief is no joke. But oh, the friends I have. No words capture that! No words capture the value of knowing, being known. No words capture how many cherished friends, old and new, came to my rescue during those moments when I wished I was gone so that I could hold Joanne one more time, or at least, say goodbye. I have the luxury in the knowledge that I can pick up the phone or show up and open, loving arms will caress me. What is better? Nothing I can imagine.

And then came love again, a new, exciting, unexpected love, a long distance love that over a year has grown, evolved, and brought balance again.

EPILOGUE
Loss, Life, Love

My greatest struggle these days is the loss of youth—the physical loss, not the intellectual or emotional. I'm over sixty now. Youth fades more quickly than one ever thinks possible, and it's a journey in itself, the gradual cues that you're less able to open bottles, see fine print, garden, wake up pain-free, and stay up past 10:00. In addition, you notice your memory just isn't what it once was. It's a journey toward that acute and inevitable awareness of mortality, of losing friends and family, a journey to the unknown, the unknown of youth toward old age. The upside is the wisdom one gains just by virtue of experiencing life, and sadly with this, death.

On October 27, 2012, my precious, stunningly beautiful, perfect, beloved wife of twenty-five years passed away suddenly, unexpectedly, and far too soon, and so quickly that I didn't get to say goodbye, to have that last conversation, kiss, or look. Eleven months later, on September 14, 2012, I sat by my mother's side as she took her last breath. No easy year, but one of reaching far into the depths of my heretofore, untouched by losses of this magnitude, life. I've known sorrow, especially in my career, but none with a sting like these.

The cruel irony of Joanne's passing was that we worked up to the very week that we left San Diego and moved back to Tucson to retire and to spend time with my aging mother. We had bought a house and, once settled, were planning the trip of our lives. Our twenty-five years together were nothing short of miraculous. What majestic, grand, adventurous, and brave love it was. Majestic and grand because of its depth—an immovable and perfect union, brave in the face of all those who regarded us as not good enough, or not valid, or hell-bound and perverse.

As for my mother, I regret that I didn't get more time with her. She and I, through years of emotional turmoil and then honest, heartfelt dialogue on both our parts, finally reached a place of calm, of mutual respect, of deep and unconditional love. I grew up! I realized that all of us, all of us only get one mother, and for better or worse, she gave us life, so precious a gift.

Words are too trite to express my gratitude for those cherished moments when friends and family reached out as welcome, loving intrusions through the past two years when I so often felt adrift and swallowed up with grief, unable to breathe some days. The loss of the two most important women in my life, the ensuing grief, and the miracle of finding love again, of finding that the emotional distance we travel from loss, grief, and devastation toward love are the tapestry of this thing called life. The exquisite surprising discovery is that moving on is possible. But the details of those two years are for a future book. For now, the eternal optimist, the woman who remains humbled by life's cruel and miraculous jaunts through time, the woman who chose to move from darkness to light is alive, so alive and ready for all the jaunts that lie ahead.

For Joanne and Mom:

You'll never get over it...it's the clichés that cause the trouble. To lose someone you love is to alter your life forever. You don't get over it because 'it' is the person you loved. The pain stops, there are new people, but the gap never closes. How could it? The particularness of someone who mattered enough to grieve over is not erased by anyone but death. The hole in my heart is in the shape of you and no one else can fit. Why would I want them to? —Jeanette Winterson, *Written on the Body*

For the rest of us:

The sky starts at your feet, think how brave you are to walk around.

ABOUT THE AUTHOR

In 1975, at the age of 21, Denise Sassoon was sentenced to "no less than five, no more than fifteen" years in the Arizona State Prison for Women. The years she spent in prison and the choices she made following her incarceration tested her resilience and her strength, awakened her heart to true love, and helped her have the courage to start healing her life's greatest wounds. Since 1988, Denise has worked continuously in some aspect of programs designed for prison reentry or drug/ alcohol treatment, including counseling clients, training counselors and support staff, managing in-house treatment programs for prison inmates, and assisting with or directing residential treatment facilities. She also helped develop pioneering programs for ex-convicts with drug and alcohol dependency issues, programs that later served as models for state-wide treatment modalities. Denise resides in her hometown of Tucson, Arizona, with her partner, Liz, and their beloved Maltese named Bentley. Denise is currently writing her second book.

Made in the USA
San Bernardino, CA
25 May 2020